I Am the Way

I am the Way

A Spiritual Journey

Through the Gospel of John

Philip Wesley Comfort

Baker Books

A Division of Baker Book House Co
Grand Rapids, Michigan 49516

Published by Baker Books
a division of Baker Book House Company
P.O. Box 6287, Grand Rapids, Michigan 49516-6287

Printed in the United States of America

Library of Congress Cataloging-in-Publication Data

Comfort, Philip Wesley.
    I am the way : a spiritual journey through the Gospel of John / Philip Wesley Comfort.
        p. cm.
    Includes bibliographical references and indexes.
    ISBN 0-8010-2591-5
    1. Bible. N. T. John—commentaries. I. Title.
BS2615.3.C626   1994
226.5'07—dc20   94-18257

Contents

Abbreviations

New Testament Greek Manuscripts Cited

P5
John 1:23–31, 33–40; 16:14–30; 20:11–17, 19–20, 22–25

P45
John 10:7–25; 10:30–11:10, 18–36, 42–57

P66
John 1:1–6:11; 6:35–14:26, 29–30; 15:2–26; 16:2–4, 6–7; 16:10–20:20, 22–23; 20:25–21:9

P75
John 1:1–11:45, 48–57; 12:3–13:1, 8–9; 14:8–30; 15:7–8

Aleph (Codex Sinaiticus)
all of John

A (Codex Alexandrinus)
all of John

B (Codex Vaticanus)
all of John

C (Codex Ephraemi Rescriptus)
John 1:4–40; 3:34–5:16; 6:39–7:2; 8:35–9:10; 11:8–46; 13:8–14:7; 16:22–18:35; 20:26–21:25

D (Codex Bezae)
all of John except 1:16–3:26; 18:13–20

T (Codex Borgianus)
John 1:24–32; 3:10–17; 4:52–5:7; 6:28–67; 7:6–8:31

W (Codex Washingtonianus)
all of John (except 1:1–5:11 supplied by later hand; and 14:26–16:7 is missing)

English Versions of the Bible

ASV	American Standard Version
KJV	King James Version
JB	Jerusalem Bible
NASB	New American Standard Bible
NEB	New English Bible
NIV	New International Version
NJB	New Jerusalem Bible
NRSV	New Revised Standard Version
REB	Revised English Bible
RSV	Revised Standard Version
TEV	Today's English Version

Other Abbreviations

LXX	Septuagint
Maj	Majority text/Majority of manuscripts
NA^{26}	*Novum Testamentum Graece*, 26th ed.
TR	Textus Receptus
UBS^4	*Greek New Testament*, United Bible Society, 4th ed.

Preface

E ach of our lives is a journey intersecting the journeys of others. Some journeys go from the womb to the tomb unnoticed. Others have left their mark. But none left so deep an impression as the journey of Jesus. His was a journey from heaven to earth and back to heaven, from glory to humility and on to greater glory. He, being God, became man. That was a journey! Then, as he journeyed this earth, he intersected the paths of many men and women. He came to them where they were and walked with them, as it were, in their shoes. His motive was to provide every person with a way out of their human predicament by giving them the light of life. To the young seekers accompanying John the Baptist, Jesus became their Teacher and Master; for those at a disappointing wedding celebration, he provided the best wine; to the perplexed and aging Nicodemus, Jesus promised a new birth; to a dissatisfied Samaritan woman, Jesus provided living water; to a hopeless, paralyzed man, Jesus gave health; to a hungry, discontent multitude, Jesus gave the bread of life; to the religious throngs in Jerusalem, Jesus promised living waters; to a blind man, Jesus became his light; to a dead man, Lazarus, Jesus gave life. Jesus provided a way for each of these people to come to God. That is why Jesus called himself "the way"—more literally "the road." That road leads to life and spiritual reality. That road leads to God. Thus, Jesus was speaking of the meaning of his existence when he said, "I am the way, the truth, and the life. No one comes to the Father except through me."

There were so many more people that Jesus touched along the way, but this Gospel gives only a few vignettes of how Jesus changed people's lives when he met them. In the closing verse of this Gospel, John said that the whole universe is not big enough to contain the books that could be written about all that Jesus said and did. The same could almost be said about John's Gospel! How many books have been written about John—enough to fill a whole library! So why should I add to the collection? Because the Fourth Gospel has intrigued me just as much as it did those thousands of others who have attempted to explain its mysteries, and because the Fourth Gospel has been my companion throughout my entire Christian journey.

I think I could do without any other book and still make it—but not John. This book has been too precious to me, too close to my life experience. And so, as I write about the spiritual journey in the Gospel of John, I include myself in that journey, as if I were one of Jesus' original followers. I encourage you to enliven your imagination and join the journey.

I trust that this volume will be useful for teachers and students of John's Gospel. Some of the thoughts in this book have been carried over from another volume I co-authored, entitled *Opening the Gospel of John*. I found it impossible in some passages to have expressed it better. In any case, I have done my best to make this work unique and to provide my readers with a new way of looking at the Fourth Gospel. Unless otherwise noted, the Bible text quoted throughout is my own translation of the Greek text.

Introduction

John was a poet; his Gospel, an elaborate poem. Its simplicity is deceptive. John specialized in double meaning, allusion, allegory, irony, and symbolism. His well-crafted work, like a symphony, advances new themes, drifts into others, then returns with similar sounds yet fresh and alluring. Most readers and commentators get lost in the sway. I have—again and again. It is difficult to step back and comprehend the greater movement of this work. But I am convinced that this book takes the reader on a designed journey led by Jesus himself and narrated by John.

And I am persuaded that this work was motivated by a writer who had been on a spiritual journey with Jesus all of his life, and was encouraging others to join him. The author had not reached his end yet; he was not exhausted or bored. He was excited about Jesus, wanted to pursue him still, and welcomed more companions on the way. If John would have titled this piece, he might have called it "My Journey with Jesus," or better yet, "Our Journey with Jesus"—for the author was very inclusive and inviting.

The book isn't just a retelling of Jesus' life and ministry. It's a story of Jesus' journey from heaven to earth to heaven, from God to flesh to Spirit—and all that he experienced along the way. It's a story of the disciples' journey with Jesus and how they struggled to find the way through him to God. And it's a story of every believer's journey with Jesus who reveals the Triune God.

The Gospel of John has been my spiritual companion for nearly twenty-five years. Hardly a day or a week has gone by that I have not meditated on this book and received nourishment from its message. Many years ago I began to realize that this Gospel was taking me with it on a journey. I, as a reader, had become a participant in a spiritual odyssey.

I began to realize that John's Gospel depicts three journeys: (1) the journey of God's Son sent by his Father to become a man living among men, then dying and rising to return to his Father in glory; (2) the journey of the disciples who followed Jesus in his journey and therein found that he was the way to God, the reality of God, and the giver of God's eternal life; and (3) the journey of all the believers who follow Jesus and the apostles on a spiritual journey that leads to full enjoyment of God. These journeys interweave throughout this Gospel because Jesus' journey from God was the means by which all the believers (the apostles and others) could know God, and Jesus' journey back to God (through death and resurrection) provided the way for all the believers to come to God through Jesus.

The purpose of the spiritual journey was for the disciples to know God the Father through the Son and Spirit. The original disciples (specifically John) had followed Jesus on a journey whose goal was to reveal to them God's true identity as incarnate in the God-man via numerous signs and oracular revelations. The purpose of the journey was also to introduce the disciples into the divine fellowship of the Father and the Son through the Spirit.

John's Gospel, unlike the Synoptic Gospels and even unlike any other book in the Bible, gives the fullest presentation of the interpersonal relationships in the Trinity—especially the Father-Son relationship, but also the Father-Son-Spirit relationship. No other book of the Bible so reveals the intimate fellowship and eternal union between the Father and the Son; no other book presents such detail about the functional relationship among the Father, Son, and Spirit. John's unveiling of the Triune God is superb, precious, and matchless. Yet even better—for our sakes, John shows how it was Jesus' primary aim to reveal the Father to those who believe and to bring them to know the Father and participate in his enjoyment of the Father, as well as enjoy their union with the Son through the Spirit.

John's Biography and the Journey Motif

Ancient and modern readers alike recognize the Gospel of John as a work of literature and value its literary worth. All four Gospels were considered "biographies" in a literary sense from as early as the second century. They were the apostolic memoirs (Greek *apŏ-nĕmoneumata*). Indeed, if we accept John the apostle's authorship of this Gospel, it is readily apparent that the Fourth Gospel is a very personal apostolic memoir written by an eyewitness—John, the son of Zebedee (see discussion below on John's authorship).

The oral proclamation of the gospel prevailed in the first two centuries of the early church and continued to exist side by side with the written Gospels well into the fourth century. When Luke mentioned the written accounts about Jesus' life that were current in the first century, he called them "narratives" (see Luke 1:1). In the middle of the second century, the word *euangelion* (good message/gospel) began to be used to describe written Gospels (Justin, *Dialogue with Trypho* 10.2; 100.1; Irenaeus, *Against Heresies* 3.1.1; Clement of Alexandria, *Stromateis* 1.21). To the early Christians, the written Gospels were accounts that contained the words and actions of Jesus; they were Jesus literature.[1]

The Gospels are a genre of their own, as distinct from the Acts of the Apostles, apocalyptic literature, epistles, and homilies. The four Gospels were also unique as literary works; nothing else in the Hellenistic world was exactly like them. The Gospels contain many literary genres—such as history, story, drama, oratory, proverb, parable, and poetry—but these genres are mingled in a way that is without exact parallel elsewhere in literature. Leland Ryken elaborates: "The uniqueness of the form known as the gospel ('good news') is obvious at once when we reflect that the form has no real parallel outside of the New Testament writings. Furthermore, none of the usual literary categories does justice to the gospels, although of course they have affinities to a number of conventional forms."[2]

The only kind of Hellenistic literature that had kinship with the Gospels would be works that were called biographical literature. In his monograph, *The New Testament in Its Literary Environment*, David Aune describes biography as follows: "Biography is a specific genre of Greco-Roman historical literature with broad generic features. Biography may be defined as a discrete prose narrative devoted exclusively to the portrayal of the whole life of a particular individual perceived as historical. It never attained a fixed form but continued to develop from ancient to modern times."[3]

Greek biography began in the fifth century B.C. with the writings of Herodotus. Other works from the fourth century have survived, such as Isocrates' *Evagoras* and Xenophon's *Education of Cyrus* and *Agesilaus*. Biographies from the first to the fourth centuries by writers such as Plutarch, Suetonius, Lucian, and Porphyry are still in existence today. Most of these ancient biographies were written with literary pretensions and display a high stylistic level in the use of vocabulary, syntax, and complex sentences of the periodic style. "The formal structure of Greco-Roman biography consists of a fundamentally chronological framework provided by a person's life (true of Suetonian as well as Plutarchan lives), amplified by anecdotes, maxims, speeches, and documents."[4] Most of these biographies were didactic in that they presented the subject as a paradigm of virtue; as a result, they tended to be encomiastic. J. A. T. Robinson observes quite accurately that "Xenophon's *Memorabilia* and Plato's *Dialogues* correspond, one can say very broadly, to the approaches respectively of the Synoptists and the Fourth Gospel."[5] Furthermore, Robinson recognizes literary parallels between the trial narrative of the Fourth Gospel and Plato's *Apology* as well as Jesus' last discourse in the Fourth Gospel and Plato's *Phaedo*.

Other biographies in the Greco-Roman world were more popular in nature, such as the *Life of Aesop,* the *Life of Homer,* the Jewish *Lives of the Prophets,* and the life of Secundus the Silent Philosopher. The four Gospels could be included in this category of biography on the basis of structure and style. The Gospels and these popular lives "exhibit a thoroughly chronological organization and avoid topical exposition." Furthermore the Gospels "reflect the popular literary culture of the lower classes. The linguistic and rhetorical style and standards of educated authors and orators of antiquity were attenuated and imitated in popular literature."[6]

Papias was a scholarly historian who collected oral and written traditions about Jesus. He described the Gospel of Mark as containing *apōnēmoneumata* (reminiscences or memoirs) drawn from Peter's sayings (*chreiai*—a term used to describe maxims illustrated by anecdotes) (Eusebius, *Church History* 3.39.15). Justin Martyr, a Christian philosopher by profession, also used the word *apōnēmoneumata* to describe the Gospels. The word *apōnēmoneumata* was a recognized literary form. According to Aune, the *apōnē-*

moneumata are "expanded chreiai, i.e., sayings and/or actions of or about specific individuals, set in narrative framework and transmitted by memory (hence 'reliable')."[7] Justin's description of the Gospels as *apōnēmoneumata* would place them in the same literary category as Xenophon's *Memorabilia* (in Greek called *apōnēmoneumata*).

The Journey Motif

It was common for ancient biographical literature to be cast in a journey or travel motif.[8] Beginning with the Homeric epic and other biblical writings (such as Abraham's story and David's story), the journey motif provided a viable way of arranging a narrative. The Gospel of John, a biographical work, is a classic example of a biographical work depicting the hero on various journeys. The journey motif is thoroughly examined by Fernando Segovia in an article entitled, "The Journeys of the Word of God." Segovia sees two aspects of this journey:

> On the one hand, the Word of God is portrayed from the very beginning of the Gospel as undertaking—at the bequest of God the Father himself—a mythological, cosmic journey from the world of God to the world of human beings, ultimately becoming flesh as Jesus of Nazareth and thus carrying out the mission of the Father in and to the world; upon the completion of this mission, the Word of God returns from the world of human beings to the world of God. As such, the cosmic journey provides an overall framework for the plot of the Gospel: the biography of Jesus of Nazareth, messiah and son of God, is the biography of the Word of God made flesh in the world. On the other hand, as the Word of God made flesh, Jesus of Nazareth is further portrayed throughout the Gospel as undertaking a series of geographical journeys in the course of his public life or ministry, thus continuing to carry out the mission of the Father in and to the world; with the completion of the last such journey, the mission itself comes to an end and the return to the world of God takes place.[9]

Segovia then constructs the narrative plot primarily based on the second aspect (i.e., the geographical) of the journey motif. The narrative plot hangs on Jesus' three journeys to Galilee (with their accompanying success) contrasted with his three journeys to Jerusalem where he met rising opposition that eventually led to his crucifixion. Segovia argues that this journey has a didactic function. It "allows Jesus, the Word of God, to engage in widespread and sustained teaching regarding the ways and values of God, his own status or identity as Word of God, and his role or mission in the world as entrusted to him by God."[10] As he travels from place to place disseminating his teachings, some people become believers and some become followers (or disciples). Thus, as both R. Alan Culpepper and J. Staley point out, the implied readers of this Gospel are indeed drawn thereby into the community of believers—initiated, confirmed, or reinforced as children of God, not only by way of repetition and recapitulation (Culpepper) but also by way of expansion and intensification (Staley).

The Gospel of John has a way of drawing its readers to follow Jesus in his journey. But contrary to Segovia's position, I think it is clear that Jesus does not make the journey back to God the Father alone. He takes the believers with him. His mission as the Word of God was to express and communicate God to humanity and then bring believing humanity into a relationship with God through him. This is characterized by Jesus' famous statement: "I am the way, the truth, and the life; no one comes to the Father except through me." Jesus had come to provide a way (a road) for the believers to travel on. Thus, the Gospel of John is not just a record of Jesus' journey but of his believers' journey.

John's Gospel reflects a personal journey for John himself, into which he draws his readers and encourages their participation. This is explicit in his first epistle, wherein he affirms his firsthand experience with "the Word of life" and then invites his readers to join him (and the other apostles, for whom he speaks) in their fellowship with the Father and the Son (see 1 John 1:1–4).

In the prologue to John's Gospel, the author uses "we" to speak of those who were the eyewitnesses of the incarnate God-man. We assume he is speaking of himself and the other apostles when he says, "and the Word became flesh and made his home among us, and *we* have seen his glory, the glory as of the only Son of the Father" (1:14). John then goes on to include his readers, saying, "and of his fullness have *we all* received, even grace upon grace." By including his readers as recipients of Jesus' bountiful supply of grace he makes them participants in the story that is about to unfold. Although the readers are not among the first followers of Jesus, they are encouraged to participate in the same spiritual journey the apostles took.

In the first chapter of John, we discover that Andrew and "the other disciple" (i.e., John) left John the Baptist to follow Jesus, the Lamb of God. According to the narrative begun in 1:29, the "third day" mentioned in 2:1 would seem to be the fourth day (day one, 1:29; day two, 1:35; day three, 1:43; day four, 2:1). But 2:1 speaks of "the third day" because that is the third day after John began to follow Jesus (1:35). Thus, the narrative is given to us in terms of a personal diary or memoir. Even if these days are not literally days, they speak of time-periods in John's journey of following Jesus.

A Spiritual Reenactment of Israel's Journey

This journey is intended not to be just a personal one or one just for the original disciples of Jesus. John wants to take all the believers on this spiritual journey—a journey that is very reflective of the journey the Israelites took from Egypt to Canaan and thereby experienced their God. The motif of Israel's salvation history was engraved on John's mind and is found everywhere in the pages of his Gospel. John's Gospel constantly reflects the exodus (accompanied by miraculous signs), the journey in the wilderness (wherein God miraculously supplies his people), and the entrance into the good land, wherein God's people establish God's kingdom and temple (in the midst of hostile enemies) as a display of God's glory. John sees himself and the disciples involved in the spiritual reenactment of this history. Jesus creates a new Israel, with a new habitation and kingdom—those that are spiritual. Only those who are born of the divine Spirit can see this kingdom and enter into it (3:3–6). In John's Gospel, Jesus is the way to God, the reality of God, and the eternal life of God (14:6). The spiritual journey takes the believer through Jesus (the Son) to God the Father.

Even though John quotes the Old Testament far less than any of the other Gospel writers (ten times to be exact: 1:51 from Gen. 28:12; 2:17 from Ps. 69:9; 12:13 from Ps. 118:25; 12:15 from Zech. 9:9; 12:38 from Isa. 53:1; 13:18 from Ps. 41:9; 19:24 from Ps. 22:18; 19:36 from Exod. 12:46; and 19:37 from Zech. 12:10), his Gospel is saturated with allusions to the Old Testament. But these allusions are not scattered; they have one thematic thrust: to show that Jesus had come to re-create a new Israel out of the old one and make this new one spiritually alive with his divine life.

John was intent on revealing Jesus as the spiritual reality of many sacred events and items in the Jews' salvation history. Jesus came to create a new Israel, a spiritual one. This Israel was a corporate entity composed of Jesus (as the head) and his believers united in him. Together, they are the habitation of God and the vine of God. For his believers, Jesus is the Spirit of life, the Passover Lamb, the smitten rock, the living waters, the light in the darkness, the manna, the serpent lifted up on the pole—and the way to God his Father. Jesus becomes a substitute for the Jewish festivals (such as Passover and Tabernacles) and the Jewish "institutions" (such as the temple and the Passover lamb).

Though John's Gospel constantly reflects the pattern of Israel's salvation history, the reader will not see it presented in an exact chronology that parallels Israel's history. During Jesus' days on earth he was all things at the same time and at any time for those who believed in him and received his words as spirit and life. Yet nearly every spiritual reality in John's Gospel awaited its full actualization in Christ's glorification through death and resurrection, at which time the Spirit of Christ was made available to the believers for their life. In other words, John's Gospel is very forward-looking—anticipating the time (called "the hour" in John) of glorification when the disciples could live in God and God in them.

All the christological types presented in Israel's salvation history find their realization and fulfillment in Jesus' glorification, which is the death/resurrection event. For believers to have life, Jesus had to die. Life comes out of death. The Lamb of God must be killed to take away the sins of the world; the true temple of God, Jesus, would be destroyed but then rise from the dead; Jesus would be lifted up on the pole to give life to those who believe in him; the bread of God must be killed as a sacrifice to give life to those who eat him; Jesus must be struck as a smitten rock before the living waters flow; the shepherd must lay down his life for his sheep to have abundant life; and the grain must fall into the ground and die before many grains can live. These are the images that Jesus used to describe how he had to die so that those who believed in him could have the divine, eternal life.

Just as the Israelites' journey had a goal—to establish God's dwelling and kingdom as a glorious testimony to the surrounding nations—so does the Christian journey have a glorious goal, which is expressed completely in Jesus' prayer in John 17, wherein he prays that the believers' unity would be realized in their living union with God and would be a testimony to the world that the Father sent his Son. Until we reach that unity, wherein the body of Christ grows into all the fullness of the head (Eph. 4:13–16), we are supplied by the head, Jesus Christ, with everything we need for our spiritual lives.

The reenactment motif is taken to a higher, spiritual level as the Gospel narrative unfolds. In a sense, the history of Israel's journey was but a foreshadowing of a journey that is realized by believers today. As the narrative continues, we see Jesus abandoning Judaism and, in its place, offering himself as the reality of all it stood for. His intention to make anew a spiritual habitation and spiritual kingdom is evident in the very first chapters of this Gospel.

In John 1 we first see that the God-man, Jesus, has come to dwell among people as God's new tabernacle. But the believers cannot yet live in him. They first need him as the Lamb of God who takes away the sins of the world; then with the blood of the Lamb they can enter into God's dwelling. In John 2 Jesus points to himself as the true temple of God to be erected on the day of his resurrection. The temple in Jerusalem is no longer inhabited by God, for it has been corrupted with merchandising—it is a den of thieves. In John 3 Jesus reveals the necessity of a corporate regeneration for the nation of Israel, a nation dead to God like the dry bones Ezekiel saw. This regeneration was a prerequisite for entrance into God's spiritual kingdom; at the same time Jesus points to himself as the one who has to be lifted up on the pole (cross) to secure Israel's salvation. In John 4 Jesus is presented as God's gift of life to the world, including the Samaritans who were the outcasts of Palestine. At the same time Jesus spoke of a new kind of worship—not in the temple, but in the spirit, for God is Spirit. God in Christ was seeking any and all people, not just the Jews, to worship him in spirit. By the time we reach John 5, it is clear that Jesus considered Israel to be as paralyzed as the man who had sat by the pool for thirty-eight years. He had come to give life to the spiritually dead.

In John 6 Jesus is presented as the true manna from heaven; in John 7, as the reality of the smitten rock. Both these images harken back to the time of Israel's journey in the wilderness. Jesus had come to bring his people on a journey into God, and Jesus would be the one who supplied them on the way. But very few continued to follow—only Twelve, and one of those was a devil and a betrayer. In John 8 Jesus is presented as the I AM WHO I AM and the light of the world—the one come to bring his chosen people out of the darkness of Judaism. In John 9, one man comes out—the man born blind healed by Jesus to gain his physical sight and spiritual vision. He recognizes Jesus as the Messiah and is subsequently expelled from Judaism. This man becomes typical of all who will leave Judaism in similar fashion. In John 10 Jesus reveals himself as the Good Shepherd of a new, united flock (composed of Jews called out of Judaism and Gentiles). By this time he had given up on Judaism, and was calling his own sheep to come out and follow their true shepherd into the pasture.

In John 11 and 12 Jesus is presented as the resurrection and the life to his people—the grain of wheat that must be buried in order to generate many grains. In John 13 he is presented as the master become servant to cleanse his people from their sins. In John 14 he is again presented as the true habitation of God prepared for the believers to live in; and in John 15 the same image is depicted, yet in this picture the habitation is organic—the believers and Jesus live in one another as branches and vine. In John 16 Jesus reveals the work and person of the Spirit as the one who continues Jesus' invisible presence in the disciples. In John 17 Jesus reveals through prayer his desires for the spiritual unity and corporate testimony of his people. In John 18 and 19, Jesus is presented as the suffering son of David and true Passover Lamb. John 20 presents the climax and culmination of the Gospel: Jesus rises from the dead and imparts the Spirit of life into his believers, thereby inaugurating the new creation. John 21 is the epilogue for this journey.

The reader of John's Gospel sees Jesus portrayed as one greater than Moses—performing signs to gain his disciples' faith, giving grace and reality surpassing even the Law. Jesus is clearly the Prophet and Messiah that Moses predicted. Further, Jesus is depicted as the One who existed before Abraham was ever born, and as the true son of David come to deliver his people. Indeed, there was an expectation among the people that the Messiah would reenact the glorious salvation history of Israel in new ways. The details of the new salvation will unfold as we explore together this journey whose ultimate goal is to bring the believers into a living relationship with the Triune God, and a loving relationship with each other, so that they together can be a corporate testimony to the world of God's grace and Christ's salvation.

The Symbolism of the Geographic Movement

According to the Synoptic Gospels, Jesus journeys from Galilee to Jerusalem only once. This intensifies the drama that leads up to the events in his final week in Jerusalem, wherein Jesus is at first hailed in his triumphal entry and then condemned to crucifixion. But John's presentation is more mimetic of reality. Jesus went to Jerusalem several times, and from the very first visit he was predicting that the Jewish leaders would kill him (see John 2:17–21). Thereafter, Jesus was increasingly persecuted every time he went to Jerusalem.

What is clear is that Jesus had completely given up on Jerusalem as the representation and embodiment of Judaistic religion. His journeys into Jerusalem usually brought about confrontation and conflict, and eventually ended in crucifixion. His journeys away from Jerusalem usually generated clarity, calm, and conversions. This is a symbolic pattern in this Gospel, which is outlined as follows:

Beyond the Jordan and in Galilee
1:19–2:12
• calling of disciples
• miracle in Cana

Jerusalem
2:13–3:21
• cleansing of the temple—prediction of Jesus' death
• Nicodemus' spiritual deadness, typifing Israel's need for regeneration

Judean countryside, Samaria, Galilee
3:22–4:54
• making more disciples in Judean countryside
• many new believers in Samaria
• second miracle in Cana

Jerusalem
5:1–47
- active persecution against Jesus begins
- healing of paralyzed man, symbolizing Israel's paralyzed condition

Galilee, near Capernaum
6:1–7:13
- purposeful avoidance of Jerusalem (6:4)
- miraculous feeding of the five thousand
- presentation of the bread of life

Jerusalem
7:14–10:39
- though some believed, Jesus' identity is severely questioned
- Jesus avoids arrest
- Jesus heals a blind man, who is excommunicated from Judaism
- the Jewish leaders on two occasions attempt to stone Jesus (8:59; 10:31)

Beyond the Jordan, Bethany, and Ephraim
10:40–12:11
- Jesus left Jerusalem and went beyond the Jordan to the place where John the Baptist was first baptizing (1:28)—many believed in him there
- Jesus went to Bethany, where he raised Lazarus from the dead
- Jesus left Judea for Ephraim (11:54)
- Jesus went to Bethany

Jerusalem
12:12–20:31
- Jesus made his triumphal entry into Jerusalem
- Jesus celebrated the Last Supper with his disciples
- Jesus was arrested, tried, and crucified
- Jesus rose from the dead and appeared to the disciples

Galilee
21:1–25

- Jesus appeared to some of his disciples as they were fishing on the Sea of Galilee

The return to Galilee at the end of the Gospel is significant inasmuch as it symbolizes a new beginning outside of Jerusalem.

A Journey into the Triune God

God the Father and the Son have always shared the same divine, eternal life and enjoyed each other's love. Then they created human beings so that they could share this life and love with them. God is glad to give the divine, eternal life to each believer and so beget many lovely and loving children. And God's heart's desire has always been to include these children in the fellowship he had always enjoyed with his one and only Son. Thus, when the Son was sent to earth, he was commissioned by the Father to explain and express him to humankind. His mission was also to bring all the believers into a life-relationship with the Father. Once people believed in the Son, they would be granted the right to become children of God (John 1:12). They then could "get to know" the Father and begin to fellowship with him through the Son. Thus, the ultimate aim of the Son's commission was to bring many people into a living, experiential relationship with the Father.

Many Christians think the Son's commission on earth was to accomplish redemption. This is true, but this was but a means to an end. The goal was to bring people back into a living relationship with God the Father by making them children of God and by providing the way for them to have fellowship with God.

The Gospel of John, unlike the Synoptic Gospels, dwells on the relationship between the Father and the Son. In this Gospel, Jesus constantly referred to his Father in the most intimate expressions. He continually referred to his preincarnate experience with the Father—speaking of those things he and his Father had seen and heard together (3:11; 8:38), even relating that he had seen the Father's visage (5:37; 6:46)! The Son also revealed that he had not really left the Father, nor the Father him, when he came to earth. The Father who sent the Son was still with the Son. Three times Jesus declared, "I am not alone: the Father who sent me is with me" (8:16, 29; 16:32). Three other times the Lord announced that he and the Father were one (10:30, 38; 14:9–10; 17:21) because they mutually indwelt each other. What intimacy! The Son and the Father loved each other dearly, and the Son repeatedly asserted that he was utterly dependent upon the Father. The Son had not come in his own name (i.e., to establish his own independent reputation), but in the name of the Father. His chief aim was to glorify the Father and to bring the believers into an experiential knowledge of him.

The disciples, however, found it difficult to conceptualize the Father Jesus so often talked about. During the Lord's final discourse with his disciples, he again spoke of the Father. Exasperated, Philip blurted out, "Show us the Father and we will be satisfied" (14:8). He thought the Father was another person that Jesus could beckon to appear in the room. But the request was impossible to satisfy because the Son is the Father seen, the Father made visible. The Son was and has always been the image of the invisible God (2 Cor. 4:4; Col. 1:15; Heb. 1:3). Jesus told Philip, "He who has seen me has seen the Father. Don't you realize that I am in the Father and the Father is in me?" (John 14:9–10 paraphrased). This was hard for Philip and the disciples to understand. The most they realized then was that Jesus had come from God (16:30). It wasn't until after their new birth that the Holy Spirit made these precious truths clear to them—especially to John. How much later? We do not know because John's writings may have been produced when he was very old, at the end of the apostolic age (ca. A.D. 90–95). The Spirit brought many things Jesus said to John's remembrance and then illuminated them. At some point in John's life, he realized who had been in their midst. Jesus was not just the Savior, or even just the Christ, but the divine Son of God, even God himself, the great I AM. And John perceived that Jesus, the God-man, was in constant concert with another—the Father. He and the Father were in continual fellowship, a fellowship that existed from eternity and was transferred into time, embodied (as it were) in a man. The fellowship did not cease due to the incarnation; it continued in a different form.

When John opened his Gospel, he fondly recollected how he (and the other disciples, for whom he was a spokesman) beheld the Son's glory, the glory as of a unique Son from a Father (1:14). And then he picturesquely described the unique Son, himself God, dwelling in the Father's bosom (1:18). The opening of John's first epistle also contains a personal testimony:

> That which was from the beginning, that which we have heard, that which we gazed upon and our hands handled, concerning the Word of life—indeed the life was manifested, and we have seen and bear witness and announce to you the eternal life that was face to face with the Father and was manifested to us—that which we have seen and heard we announce also to you that you also may have fellowship with us; and our fellowship is with the Father and with his Son, Jesus Christ.

The first words may strike us as odd. Instead of saying, "He who was from the beginning, he whom we have seen, etc.," he wrote, "that which [a relative pronoun] was from the beginning, that which we have seen, and etc." I believe John did this because the relative pronoun is more inclusive: it encompasses everything concerning the Word of life, everything pertaining to (Greek *peri*) the Word of life from the beginning. It includes the Word's person and his work. It must also include that eternal fellowship that existed between the Word and the Father. (*Note:* as in John 1:1, he talks about the Word being face to face with the Father.) The Word of life, who was face to face with the Father, was manifested to the disciples. John heard, saw, beheld, and even handled the One who was in fellowship with the Father.

When the Son entered into time, that eternal fellowship also entered into time. Thus, to have heard Jesus was to have heard the Father speaking in the Son (14:10, 24), to have seen Jesus was to have seen the Father (14:8–10), and to have known him was to have known him who was one with the Father (10:30, 38). As was noted earlier, he and the Father were so united they indwelt each other. If this is too mysterious to comprehend, imagine a very mature Christian, one who walks in union with Christ. To know this spiritual Christian is to know a person who is completely absorbed with another person, Christ—so much so, that to know the Christian is to know Christ. Of course, this analogy cannot be taken too far because there is no single Christian who perfectly expresses Christ. That is for Christ's Body to fulfill. But Christ himself perfectly expressed the Father because he lived in perfect union with him. For the disciples to know Jesus was for them to know the Father.

During the days of his ministry, Jesus was introducing the Father to the disciples and initiating them into the fellowship. Then once the disciples were regenerated by the eternal life, they actually entered into fellowship with the Father and the Son. Having been brought into this divine participation, the apostles became the new initiators—introducing this fellowship to others and encouraging them to enter into fellowship with them. Whoever would enter into the fellowship with the apostles would actually be entering into their fellowship with the Father and the Son.

In summary, the one, unique fellowship between the Father and the Son began in eternity, was manifest in time through the incarnation of the Son, was introduced to the apostles, and then through the apostles was extended to each and every believer. When a person becomes a child of God (through the new life given by the Holy Spirit), he enters into this one ageless, universal fellowship—a fellowship springing from the Godhead, coursing through the apostles, and flowing through every genuine believer who has ever been or will ever be.

Jesus and the Spirit

Believers could never participate in living fellowship with the Father and the Son without experiencing the Holy Spirit. With the reception of the Spirit came the reception of life. But the Spirit was not made available to the believers until Jesus was glorified.

Revelation is progressive in the Gospel of John. John does not tell us from the beginning that people could not actually receive the eternal life until the hour of Christ's glorification. Throughout the Gospel, Jesus declares to various people that he can give them the eternal life if they will believe in him. He promises them the water of life, the bread of life, and the light of life, but no one could fully partake of these until after the Lord's resurrection. As a foretaste, as a sample, they could receive a certain measure of life via the Lord's words because his words were themselves spirit and life (6:63); but it was not until the Spirit would become available that the believers could actually become the recipients of the divine, eternal life. After the Lord's discourse in John 6 (a discourse that was very troubling and offensive to most of his disciples), Jesus said, "It is the Spirit that gives life; the flesh profits nothing" (v. 63).

In the flesh Jesus could not give them the bread of life, but when the Spirit became available, they could have life. Again, Jesus offered the water of life—even life flowing like rivers of living water—to the Jews assembled at the Feast of Tabernacles. He told them to come and drink of him. But no one could, then and there, come and drink of him. So John added a note: "But this he spoke concerning the Spirit, for the Spirit was not yet because Jesus was not yet glorified" (7:39). Once Jesus would be glorified through resurrection, the Spirit of the glorified Jesus would be available for people to drink. In John 6, Jesus offered himself as the bread of life to be eaten; and in John 7, he offered himself as the water of life to refresh. But no one could eat him or drink him until he became spirit—as was intimated in John 6:63 and then stated plainly in John 7:39.

In John 14:16–18, Jesus went one step further in identifying himself with the Spirit. He told the disciples that he would give them another Comforter. Then he told them that they should know who this Comforter was because he was, then and there, abiding with them and would, in the near future, be in them. Who else but Jesus was abiding with them at that time? Then, after telling the disciples that the Comforter would come to them, he said, "I am coming to you." First he said that the Comforter would come to them and abide in them, and then in the same breath he said that he would come to them and abide in them (see 14:20). In short, the coming of the Comforter to the disciples was one and the same as the coming of Jesus to the disciples. R. C. Moberly says, "it is not for an instant that the disciples are to have the presence of the Spirit instead of having the presence of the Son. To have the Spirit is to have the Son."[11] The Comforter who was dwelling with the disciples that night was the Spirit in Christ; the Comforter who would be in the disciples (after the resurrection) would be Christ in the Spirit.

On the evening of the resurrection, the Lord Jesus appeared to the disciples and then breathed into them the Holy Spirit. This inbreathing, reminiscent of God's breathing into Adam the breath of life (Gen. 2:7), became the fulfillment of all that had been promised and anticipated earlier in John's Gospel. Through this impartation, the disciples became regenerated and indwelt by the Spirit of Jesus Christ. This historical event marked the genesis of the new creation. Jesus could now be realized as the bread of life, the water of life, and the light of life. The believers now possessed his divine, eternal, risen life. From that time forward, Christ as Spirit indwelt his believers. Thus, in his first epistle John could say, "And hereby we know that he abides in us, by the Spirit whom he gave to us" (3:24); and again, "Hereby we know that we abide in him and he in us, because he has given us of his Spirit" (4:13). Christ is in us because his Spirit is in us. What a precious truth!

The apostles had quite an adjustment to make after Christ's resurrection. They had become so accustomed to his physical presence that it was difficult for them to learn how to live by his spiritual, indwelling presence. All through the forty days after his resurrection, from the time the apostles received the inbreathing of the Spirit, Christ was teaching the disciples to make the transfer. He would physically appear and then disappear intermittently. It seems that his aim was to guide the apostles into knowing him in his invisible presence. His desire was to help them live by faith and not by sight. When he appeared to the disciples as they were all together the second time, with Thomas present, he chided Thomas for his unbelief. Then he pronounced this blessing, "Blessed are those who do not see me and yet believe" (John 20:29).

John's Gospel: The Memoir of John, the Apostle

The narrator of this journey also participated in the journey. He was an eyewitness of Jesus and among the very first to follow Jesus. The position taken in this book is that this narrator was John, the son of Zebedee. There are several scholars who would disagree with this, and several who would agree. This book is not the proper forum for discussing the authorship of the Fourth Gospel; the major commentaries do this very adequately.

For this book John's authorship is assumed because an eyewitness account suits the journey motif of this Gospel. John himself, as one of the first disciples, ventured on that journey of following Jesus and thereby discovered a personal relationship with the Triune God. And this is the journey that he encourages his readers to experience.

Though John's authorship is not explicitly stated anywhere in the Gospel, the text itself points to his authorship. The writer of this Gospel calls himself "the one whom Jesus loved" (13:23; 19:26; 20:2; 21:7, 20); he was one of the twelve disciples, and among them he was one of those who was very close to Jesus (for example, see 13:23–25, where John is said to have been leaning on Jesus' chest during the last supper). From the Synoptic Gospels we realize that three disciples were very close to Jesus: Peter, James, and John. Peter could not have been the author of this Gospel because the one who named himself as "the one whom Jesus loved" communicated with Peter at the last supper (13:23–25), raced Peter to the empty tomb on the morning of the resurrection (20:2–4), and walked with Jesus and Peter along the shore of Galilee after Jesus' appearance to them after the resurrection (21:20–23). Thus, someone other than Peter authored this Gospel. And that someone could not have been James, for he was martyred many years before this Gospel was written (see Acts 12:2). That someone must have been John, who shared an intimate relationship with Jesus. Most likely, it was also John who was "the other disciple"—the one who with Andrew (Peter's brother) was the first to follow Jesus (1:35–40), and the one who was known to the high priest and therefore gained access for himself and Peter into the courtyard of the place where Jesus was on trial (18:15–16). This one, "the disciple whom Jesus loved," stood by Jesus during his crucifixion (19:25–26) and walked with Jesus after his resurrection (21:20). This is the same disciple who wrote the Gospel that bears his name (21:24–25). (See B. F. Westcott, who follows a similar line of reasoning to prove John's authorship.)

The question remains: Why didn't John identify himself directly? Why, instead, would he call himself "the disciple whom Jesus loved" or "the/that other disciple"? The former expression seems a bit arrogant—after all, didn't Jesus love the other disciples? Of course. But John wanted his readers to know that he had a special relationship with Jesus—not for the sake of boasting but for the sake of affirming the trustworthiness of his testimony. As the Son "in the bosom of the Father" was the one qualified to explain the Father to humankind because of his special relationship with the Father (1:18), so John, who reclined on Jesus' chest, was qualified to explain Jesus and his message to his readers because of his intimate relationship with Jesus. In this Gospel "the beloved disciple" or "the other disciple" is given a certain preeminence. If John named himself in every instance, he would have been quite arrogant. Rather, he attempted to retain some humility by referring to himself in the third person; at the same time, he probably expected his readers to clearly identify him as the apostle John and to believe in the validity of his written account.

John's authorship (whether as actual writer or authority behind the writing) of the Fourth Gospel is critical to categorizing it as an apostolic memoir. Whatever modern critics think of this issue, it is virtually certain that ancient readers—orthodox, heterodox, and heretical alike—considered the Gospel to have been written by John. The earliest solid evidence of this historical perception about the Fourth Gospel comes from P66, dated around 150, for the inscription of this manuscript ascribes the authorship to John: "Gospel according to John." Assuming that this inscription was not invented by the scribe of P66 but merely copied from another manuscript, we can imagine that John's name was being put to this work as early as 120. P75, another early manuscript containing John, which has been dated between 150 and 175, is also entitled "Gospel according to John."

John's Readers: Participants in the Journey

In recent years various scholars have tried to identify the original Johannine community—the group of believers for whom John wrote the Gospel and who were among the first to read it. That there was a Johannine community seems evident from the way John speaks *to* them and *of* them in his three epistles. The apostle John and the believers knew each other well, and the believers accepted the teachings of the apostle as "truth." John encourages them to stay in fellowship with him (and the other apostles); if they do, they will enjoy true fellowship with the Father and the Son (see 1 John 1:1–4).

In the Gospel this link between the believers and John and Jesus is also made evident. Throughout the Gospel John lets his readers know that he had a special reiationship with Jesus and was thus qualified to explain Jesus and his message to his readers. Because of his relationship to Jesus, John's testimony to his community could be trusted.

Culpepper attempted to reconstruct some of the distinctives of this Johannine community. He conjectured that this community was a kind of school (Greek *scholē*) that claimed Jesus as its founder and John as its master-teacher. This school studied the Old Testament and was reared on the teachings of John about Jesus, therein absorbing John's esoteric language about mystical experiences with Jesus. This school also collaborated with John in producing his written Gospel. As a community, they were detached from Judaism (perhaps several of the members were ex-synagogue members who were expelled for their faith in Jesus), and they struggled with false teachers who denied Jesus as the God-man. These distinctives emerged from Culpepper's close reading of the text.[12]

Then Culpepper did another study of John's Gospel based on theories of reader-reception. Adopting Wolfgang Iser's model of the implied reader, Culpepper was able to sketch the general character of John's intended readers by what information (or lack thereof) the author supplied in the narrative concerning characters, events, language, cultural practices, and so forth. According to Culpepper's study, John's intended readers are expected to already know most of the characters in the book (with the exception of the beloved disciple, Lazarus, Nicodemus, Caiaphas, and Annas). The readers should know the general regions where the stories take place, although they are unfamiliar with the specific locations—for which the author supplies some details. Thus, the readers are not from Palestine. As would be expected, the readers know Greek but not Hebrew or Aramaic. The author assumed that his readers used a Roman (not a Jewish) system of keeping time, and had little knowledge of Jewish festivals and rituals. However, the readers were expected to know the Old Testament Scriptures and to understand messianic expectations. On the whole, it seems that the readers were not Jewish but Hellenistic Christians who would have been already familiar with many parts of the Gospel story.[13]

Many scholars, including Culpepper, think John intended his Gospel to go to an existing Christian community that he had established. At the same time, just as many scholars argue that John's Gospel was intended for a greater Hellenistic audience. C. H. Dodd suggests that John was written on two levels so that the insider (a member of the Johannine community) could grasp the significance of the Gospel from each episode, while the outsiders would find its meaning gradually revealed to them step by step.[14]

What is clear is that John's Gospel was intended for a Christian audience. The Gospel's statement of purpose, plot, characterization, comments, misunderstandings, irony, and symbolism all work together in leading the reader to accept the evangelist's understanding of Jesus as the divine revealer and to share in the evangelist's concept of authentic faith, faith that certifies the believer as one of God's children.[15]

When John wrote his Gospel narrative, his primary aim was for the readers to keep on believing in Jesus as the Christ, the Son of God, and to keep on having life in his name (20:31). His Gospel was written primarily to those who already believed yet needed their faith infused with a fresh breath of life and strengthened by a clear presentation of Jesus Christ, the Son of God. (The verb tense for "believe," a present subjunctive in the earliest manuscripts containing John 20:31, indicates that John wrote this Gospel to encourage ongoing faith, more than to produce initial faith—though it can certainly do the latter quite well. The other verbal expressions in John 20:31—"believing" and "have life"—are also in the present tense, emphasizing continual action.) John's Gospel was written to encourage ongoing faith and participation in Christ's life. As Raymond Brown puts it: "The evangelist wants the believer to realize that he already possesses eternal life, that he is already a son of God, and has already met his judge. . . . The major purpose of the Gospel, then, is to make the believer see existentially what this Jesus in whom he believes means in terms of life."[16]

Since John is a Gospel, it should also be affirmed that John's book was written to spread the gospel. Those who had never heard of Jesus could read this book and find the way to eternal life. Indeed, John's narrative is set in a format that should not have been too unfamiliar to Greek readers, for all the Hellenists knew Homer's *Iliad* and *Odyssey* and Plato's *Socrates*. Jesus is the true, nonfictitious "hero" battling the alien forces of darkness on his voyage back to the Father, and Jesus is the true "philosopher" teaching his disciples in a peripatetic fashion the wisdom of God and the way to God. Hellenists reading John's Gospel would have been attracted to Jesus and perhaps realized that his mission extended beyond the Jews to the whole Hellenistic world. As such, John's Gospel would have come to them as gospel in a somewhat familiar literary setting.

1

Prologue to the Journey

John 1:1–18

reek readers of epics and biographies were very familiar with prologues. Homer's *Iliad* and *Odyssey*, two very popular works in John's day, begin with well-crafted prologues. The prologue to John's Gospel is also a literary masterpiece; it is the only true prologue in the New Testament.

A good prologue should set the tone and mood for the book; furthermore, it should entice. John's simple poetic style does just this. Indeed, the prologue has been considered by many commentators to be a poem or, at least, rhythmical prose. Some commentators have thought that verses 1–5, 10–12, and 14–18 may have been parts of one or several early Christian hymns.[1] Others have thought that verses 14–18 may have come from a kind of church confessional or corporate testimonial, of which John took the lead to confess.[2] Whatever his sources, John crafted a beautiful poem—sublime in its simplicity and yet profound in its complexity. As with all poems, the language is compacted with double meanings, metaphors, and allusions.

In the prologue we are introduced to the key themes that follow in the narrative: the Word, God, life, light, darkness, witness, the world, rejection/reception, belief, regeneration (becoming a child of God), incarnation (the Word become flesh), the one and only Son of the Father, glory, grace, truth, and fullness—all these expanded upon and illustrated in the rest of the Gospel. And we are introduced to the key figures in the Gospel: God, the Word

(Jesus, the Son of God), John the Baptist, Moses, the writer (as a spokesperson for the apostles), and all the believers.

The prologue is divided into three sections (vv. 1–5; vv. 6–13; vv. 14–18), each of which could be considered a poem by itself. All of these sections have parallel movement. They speak of the Word coming to be life and light to humankind, and then they speak of the Word being rejected and/or received.

> 1:1–5: the Word—coming as life and light to men—rejected by those in darkness
>
> 1:6–13: the Light—coming into the world—rejected by most/received by some
>
> 1:14–18: the Word—incarnated as God's tabernacle among men—received and enjoyed by his devoted followers

Each section builds upon the other and intensifies the movement. At first, the Word is rejected by his own creation. Then, he is rejected by his own people yet received by some. Finally, he is recognized by a few as God-incarnate, and they have full appreciation and enjoyment of his glory and grace.

Overall, the prologue is even arranged like the rest of the Gospel. The first part of the prologue roughly corresponds to the narrative in the sense that both deal with Jesus' public ministry, a ministry of giving life and light in the face of constant rejection. And the second part of the prologue corresponds to the private ministry of Jesus to his loved ones, in which he manifests his glory to them, gives them grace upon grace, and explains the Father to them.

Furthermore, the entire prologue presents the major steps in the Word's journey: from eternity (as God with God), to incarnation (as man among men), to reunion (as Son with his Father). Along the route, the Word brings the message of the Father to humankind, which is largely rejected but received by some who follow Jesus and thereby are brought into a relationship with the Father through his Son.

The First Movement (1:1–5)

The first five verses of the prologue constitute a kind of miniprologue. These verses contain most of the key elements found in the rest of the prologue, and span the time frame from eternity, to creation, to the Word's journey on earth, to the present (note the present tense verb in verse 5, "the light is shining"). The rest of the prologue presents the three major phases in the journey of the Word and those who followed him.

If John intended his readers to think of the beginning before all beginnings, then John 1:1 speaks of "the Word's" life before he came to earth.[3] This was a common device in Greek prologues because they functioned to provide readers with historical information about the hero before the narrative began. However, if John intended the first verse to be an incipit title, then it could be argued that John 1:1 does not describe the preincarnate Son of God, but Jesus Christ, the God-man.[4] Since the prologue is poetry, we must allow for both meanings.

In any case, the prologue sets the stage for the journey of the Word and the accompanying journey of the disciples. In the first five verses we are introduced to the main character of this biographical journey: he is called "the Word" because he is the perfect and complete expression of deity. And we are told that, before coming to earth, the Word lived in the beginning with God and was himself God. This is a paradox beyond explanation: How can one be with God and yet also be God? What we gather from the first verse is that the Word (who is both the Son of God and God)[5] lived in face-to-face fellowship with God his Father.[6] The final verse of the prologue (v. 18) tells us that the Son was in the bosom of the Father, and in Jesus' intercessory prayer (John 17) he revealed that the Father loved him before the foundation of the world. We cannot imagine the extent of their union and communion.

The Word's first act was to work with God in creating the universe.[7] His second great act was to come to men as the light of life. The essential nature of the Word is life (Greek, *zōē*), and this life gives light to men who live in darkness. The divine life resided in Christ, and he made it available to all who believe in him. Human beings are born with the natural life—called *psuchē* in Greek (translated "soul," personality," or "life"); they do not possess the eternal life. The divine life can be received only by believing in the one who possesses it—Jesus Christ.

The divine life embodied in Christ illuminated the inner lives of the people he came in contact with.[8] Light is the emanation of the divine, eternal life embodied in Jesus Christ; light is life reaching and penetrating people—illumining them (as to the divine truth) and exposing them (as to their sin). Everywhere Christ was present, he gave light—light to reveal his identity and light to expose sin (see 3:21; 8:12).

Christ shone in the midst of a darkened humanity—and he continues to shine. But "the darkness did not grasp it." The Greek verb *katalambanō* can mean "grasp" or "conquer." In a poetic text, the author can intend both meanings. The darkness did not grasp or comprehend the light, and yet it also did not "extinguish it" (TLB). The NEB uses the word "mastered" to convey both ideas. This statement indicates that there has been a struggle between the darkness and the light. The darkness—unregenerate humankind under the influence of Satan, the prince of darkness—has not accepted the light and even resists the light. But the light prevails!

The Second Movement (1:6–13)

The struggle between light and darkness is elaborated in the next six verses (6–11). The Word's forerunner, John the Baptist, had come to bear witness to the light, but the light was rejected. Those who rejected Jesus remained in the darkness. This is the low point of the prologue (vv. 10–11): the very Word who participated in the creation was rejected by his own creation; the Messiah was unrecognized by his very own people.

John the Baptist "was sent from God" to prepare the way for the journey of the Word among human beings. John the Baptist is given a prominent position in the prologue because his ministry ushered in the messianic age. He was instrumental in pointing the people to Jesus the Messiah. In fact, John the Gospel writer was a disciple of John the Baptist but then left him after he pointed the way to the Lamb of God (1:36–37).

John the Baptist was a vehicle through which people could come to believe in Christ. The greatest man ever born (John the Baptist) had the highest privilege: he was a witness to Christ and a medium through whom people could believe in Christ. The writer made it clear that no one was to believe in John the Baptist because "he was not the light." Even so, when the Light came into the world,[9] he was rejected. The Jews did not welcome Jesus. How sad—even how tragic—that Jesus was not recognized by his very own people and was not welcomed by them. As a nation, they rejected their Messiah.

Beginning with verse 12 the prologue makes its ascent out of the depths of dark dejection. Not all rejected the Light. There were some who believed in Jesus, and they became the children of God. These were the ones who experienced a new spiritual birth—they were "born of God" (v. 13). To these regenerated ones the rest of the prologue is addressed, for only they could understand what it is to receive Jesus' abundant supply of grace and truth.

The Third Movement (1:14–18)

Speaking on behalf of the disciples, John says that they were those who realized that "the Word had become flesh"—that God had become a man.[10] Elsewhere John said that they "touched, heard, and gazed upon this Word of life" (1 John 1:1–2). They were the ones who recognized that God had commenced a monumental journey by becoming a man to live among men. God became what he never was before—a man, a human being. Yet when he became a man he did not cease being God. He was both God and man, the God-man. This happened when "the Word became flesh."

Speaking of the God-man's presence among men, John wrote "he tabernacled among us" or "he pitched his tent among us." To the Greek reader familiar with the Old Testament, this would have readily brought to mind the Old Testament tabernacle. The next words ("and we have seen his glory") would have especially emphasized this association, for the tabernacle was filled with the shekinah glory of God (see Exod. 40:34). The tabernacle in the wilderness was temporary and outwardly unattractive; it was, nevertheless, God's dwelling place among men, the place where God met man and man met God. Jesus was God's new tabernacle among men. God, in Jesus, dwelt among men. What a thought! The man living with the disciples was God incarnate! In Christ God came to meet with man; through Christ men could come to meet with God. Jesus, like the tabernacle, may have been outwardly unattractive; but inwardly he contained the shekinah glory of God.

The image of the tabernacle also speaks of God's presence accompanying the believers in their spiritual journey. God told the

Israelites when they were in the wilderness, "I will dwell among them and walk among them" (Lev. 26:12; cf. 2 Cor. 6:16). Wherever God's people went, the tabernacle went—and there was God's presence among them. Throughout the Gospel of John, Jesus brought God's presence to the believers. As they traveled with Jesus, God traveled with them.

The God who dwelt in the tabernacle of old had now come to dwell among men—in a man, Jesus. And John was among those who saw the glory—the glory of the one and only Son. They were attracted and began to follow this tabernacle on an incredible journey that would eventually lead them into the very glory that inhabited Jesus, the glory of God himself. Along the way, the sojourners would experience Jesus providing them with the spiritual sustenance necessary for the journey. He would be their spiritual manna and give them water from the spiritual rock. Since John and the other disciples had partaken of this full supply, he could say, by experience, that God's Son was "full of grace and spiritual reality."

Near the end of the prologue, John speaks of Moses and Jesus. He does so because he wants his readers to realize that a new leader, Jesus, had come to lead his people on a journey into the realities of God. Moses was the leader of the Jews on their journey from Egypt through the wilderness on the way to Canaan. Jesus is the new Moses who came to lead his people out of the darkened world into the light of God. Moses had given the people "the law." This law, as an expression of God's character, was intended to show man that he should live a life reflecting God's nature. But man could not and cannot do this because of his fallen nature and indwelling sin. But God incarnate, Jesus Christ, lived a life fulfilling all the righteous requirements of the law. In addition, Christ provided something Moses could not provide: grace and truth (or, reality). And this "grace and truth" was not something Christ gave as a kind of commodity detached from himself; he was the embodiment and conveyor of grace and truth. As the NASB puts it, "grace and truth were realized through him."

But it was not just the apostles who had partaken of Christ's full supply of grace and truth. All the believers have. This is why John exclaims, "and *we all* have received from his fullness, even grace added to grace." The words "we all" refer to all the believers, not just John and the apostles (for whom he was spokesman—1:14).

Thus, John explicitly includes all his readers and makes them co-participants in the apostles' experience of Jesus. In no other Gospel are the readers so included.

John concludes his prologue by saying, "No man has seen God at any time; the unique One, himself God,[11] who dwells in the bosom of the Father, has explained him." At first glance, this verse seems out of context; but it thematically follows verse 17 and provides an excellent conclusion to the entire prologue. The statement, "no one has seen God at any time," recalls what God said to Moses in Exodus 33:20. Moses wanted to see the God who had called his people on this journey through the wilderness (Exod. 33:18), but he was not allowed to gaze directly upon God's glory; God told him that no man could see God and live. This, therefore, continues the contrast between Moses and Jesus (begun in v. 17). Moses, a man, was among those mortals who could not see God. Jesus, God's Son, even God himself, lived in the presence of the Father. In 6:46 Jesus said that no one has seen the Father except he who is of God—this one has seen the Father. Only the Son, who is himself God, has seen God and can communicate his glory to men (see comments on 1:14).

The next phrase is extremely significant. John concludes the prologue with picturesque language portraying the Son as a child in close dependence on his Father—enjoying comforting communion with him, for the Son is "in the bosom of the Father." It also reflects the image of two companions enjoying fellowship during a meal. According to an ancient custom, the one who reclined next to the master at a meal was the one dearest to him. (See Luke 16:23 for an example of a similar depiction—Lazarus in the bosom of Abraham; and see John 13:23 for a description of John reclining on the bosom of Jesus.) In short, the image depicts closeness, comfort, and intimate companionship.

This description, echoing the expression "the Word was face to face with God" in 1:1, could be a timeless one—that is, it describes the Son's constant relationship with the Father as it has always been and will ever be. But, given the journey motif, this language describes a reunion of the Son with his Father at the end of the Word's journey. And what better way to celebrate the reunion than by a feast! This is the reunion that Jesus looked forward to throughout his days on earth and the reunion that he asked for in his final prayer to the Father (see John 17:1–5, 24–26). In this reunion Jesus recaptured his former glory.

The Son had accomplished his mission, he had come to explain God the Father to humankind; as the final statement of the prologue says, "he has explained him."[12] In context, this tells us that the Son is God's explainer, God's explicator, even God's exegete. It also tells us that Jesus came to narrate God—to lead us on a tour into the realities of God. Christ came to narrate God to us and to explain God to us, with words and by his very person. Technically, John is the narrator of the Gospel, but Jesus is the narrator John's narration points to, for Jesus is God's explainer. Again, this mirrors 1:1, in which the Son is called "the Word," that is, the expression of God, the communicator of God.

The prologue begins and ends on the same theme; verses 1 and 18, in effect, mirror each other. In both verses the Son is called "God," the Son is depicted as the expression ("the Word") and explainer of God, and the Son is shown in intimate fellowship with the Father—"face to face with God" and "in the bosom of the Father."

Being the First Followers in the Journey

John 1:19—2:12

J ohn's narrative begins with a presentation of Jesus' forerunner, John the Baptist, and a description of those who first followed Jesus: John (the Gospel writer), Andrew, Peter, Philip, and Nathanael. As the forerunner, John's function was to prepare "the way of the Lord." This way, like a road, needed to be made ready for the Lord's coming. The Lord had come on a journey from heaven to earth to live among and in humans. The human soul had to be ready to receive this heavenly Sojourner. Those who accepted this Sojourner would then join him in his journey.

Jesus' first followers were attracted to him after John the Baptist introduced him as the Lamb of God (a key symbol for Israel's deliverance prior to the exodus). These men were convinced, through the reading of Scripture and the testimony of others, that Jesus was the awaited Messiah. From the onset, they had incredible revelations about Jesus, because these men were seekers whose hearts were prepared to receive the Lord. They realized that Jesus was the Christ, the Son of God, and the King of Israel, and they were promised that they would see even greater things from the Revealer of God's glory.

Jesus' Forerunner, John the Baptist (1:19–34)

John the Baptist figures greatly in the journey, because his task was to prepare the way of the Lord (v. 23). He did not claim to be the Christ, Elijah, or the Prophet (vv. 19–21). It is easy to understand that he was not the Christ, but since the Old Testament predicted that Elijah would come to prepare the way for the Messiah (Mal. 3:1; 4:5–6), why did John the Baptist say he wasn't Elijah? This is a mystery. Jesus' words on this only add to the enigma because Jesus said that John was the predicted Elijah, if the Jews had accepted him (see Matt. 11:14; 17:10–12). Yet the angel speaking to Zechariah said that John would come "in the spirit and power of Elijah" (Luke 1:17). So, was John Elijah or not? John himself said he wasn't. Perhaps John did not know he was the Elijah. Or perhaps John was just being consistent with his desire to avert attention from himself to Christ; thus, to claim to be Elijah would be to draw attention to himself and away from Christ. Whether or not John was Elijah or he had come in the spirit of Elijah is not fully clarified in the New Testament, but his role and demeanor were truly Elijah-like (cf. 2 Kings 1).

It is less difficult to understand why John denied being "the Prophet" (see Deut. 18:15–18) because, whereas the Jews thought "the Prophet" and "the Messiah" were two separate figures, Jesus was both the Messiah and the Prophet (Acts 3:20–22).

John the Baptist saw himself as the Messiah's forerunner and herald. He didn't say this, but it is implicit in his self-identification: "I am the voice of one calling in the desert, Make straight the way of the Lord" (John 1:23). This is a quotation from Isaiah 40:3, a portion of Scripture that introduces the Messiah's forerunner and herald. In Isaiah 40:3–11 the herald is pictured as announcing the coming of the divine Shepherd. So, without directly telling the Jews who he was, John indicated he was heralding the Messiah's coming. In ancient times, the function of a herald was to go before a dignitary, announcing his coming and clearing the way before him. John was doing just that. Yet surprisingly, John did not see himself as being that important; he was merely a voice, calling upon people to make themselves ready for the coming One.

This is the first time in the Gospel that "the way" is mentioned; it marks the course for the journey. This journey goes two ways: it is the Lord's journey into people's hearts and it is the people's journey to discover the Lord. This ambivalence is even inherent in the expression "the way of the Lord"; as an objective genitive it can give the sense "the way to the Lord" or as a subjective genitive it can mean "the Lord's way." Both are right and probably intended in the poetics of this prophecy.

John was a road-paver, a preparer and forger of the way. In his role as a forerunner, John prepared the road for the Messiah by helping people get ready spiritually. John called upon the people to make the crooked places straight, to fill in the valleys, and to level the hills. This spiritual roadwork was accomplished by repentance and water baptism. Historically, Gentiles converting to Judaism were baptized as a purification and initiation rite. Now, John was calling upon Jews to be baptized. In saying this, John may have been referring to Ezekiel 36:25–27—God's promise to cleanse his people (with water) from their sins and then to give them new hearts filled with his Spirit. It was John's function to administer the sign of repentance; it would be Jesus' function to provide the people with new hearts and a new Spirit.

John, the herald, prepared the way for Jesus by announcing him as "the Lamb of God who takes away the sin of the world" (1:29). To every listening Jew, the title "Lamb of God" would have been pregnant with meaning; it would have reminded them of the lambs used in the daily sacrifices for the sin offerings (Lev. 14:12–13, 21, 24; Num. 6:12) and of the messianic lamb led to the slaughter (Isa. 53:7–10). More than anything, it would have recalled the Passover lamb (Exod. 12; cf. John 19:36) and evoked the image of Israel's deliverance from bondage.

In saying that Jesus was the Lamb of God, John was declaring that Jesus was the substitutionary sacrifice provided by God. He was also intimating that the announced Messiah came, not to be a conqueror, but a suffering Savior and a Deliverer. He came to do what we could not do for ourselves—take away sin.[1] As the antitype of the Passover lamb, Jesus would provide for all believers the means for being delivered from sin. And just as the eating of the Passover lamb marked the beginning of Israel's journey, so the reception of Jesus as the Lamb of God marks the beginning of every believer's journey. Indeed, this is where the first followers of Jesus began (see comments below).

The slain lamb also symbolizes the first step in the worship of God. Without the shedding of blood, the priests could not approach God's presence. For Jesus to be initially presented as the Lamb of God shows that God wanted to provide the way for believers to approach him. The shed blood of the Lamb takes care of the sin that separates people from God. With the separation removed, people can approach God to worship him and commune with him.

John the Baptist was convinced that Jesus was the awaited Messiah when he baptized Jesus, for it was at this baptism that John saw the Holy Spirit descend upon Jesus (1:32–33). In a well-known messianic passage, the Messiah is depicted as having the sevenfold Spirit resting upon him (Isa. 11:1–2). Another passage, Isaiah 61:1–3a, also pictures the Messiah as being anointed with the Spirit of the Lord God. This endowment with the Holy Spirit was a manifest sign of Jesus' messiahship. Hereafter, throughout his ministry Jesus would live and work in full dependence upon the Holy Spirit (Luke 4:14, 18).

Furthermore, Jesus would baptize believers with the Holy Spirit. Jesus came to immerse people in the Holy Spirit, and thereby make available to them the divine life. Throughout this Gospel, Jesus is presented as the divine life-giver; he came to give the divine life to those who believe in him and receive him.

Convinced that Jesus was the Messiah, John proclaimed, "I myself have seen and have testified that this is the chosen One of God" (1:34, NEB). This reading (as opposed to the reading "the Son of God")[2] suits the context well because Isaiah 42:1 predicts that God will put his Spirit on his "chosen One." John, who had just witnessed Jesus being anointed with the Spirit, made one more declaration about the Messiah, which fulfilled yet another prophecy of Isaiah.

Jesus' First Disciples Begin the Journey (1:35–51)

John, the Gospel writer, kept a journal of the days he first saw Jesus and followed him. The first day was when he heard John the Baptist proclaim Jesus as "the Lamb of God who takes away the sin of the world" (v. 29). The next day was when the Baptist made the same proclamation, prompting John and Andrew to follow Jesus (vv. 35–36). The next day covers the story about Jesus finding Philip and Philip bringing Nathanael to Jesus (vv. 43–51). Then, John mentions "the third day" in 2:1. This "third day" had to have been the third day of John following Jesus. It may not have been a period of seventy-two hours; rather, "three days" may have sig-naled three time-segments in the early events of the journey.

The First Day of the Journey (1:35–42)

This portion of John shows how the earliest believers became Jesus' followers and embarked on the greatest of all spiritual jour-neys. Andrew and John (the Gospel writer) became Jesus' follow-ers through the testimony of their teacher, John the Baptist. Peter, Andrew's brother, became a follower through the testimony of Andrew. Peter and Andrew probably told Jesus about Philip, who became the fourth disciple of Jesus. Philip then told Nathanael about Jesus, and he became the fifth disciple. Quite possibly, the first five disciples, John, Andrew, Peter, Philip, and Nathanael, were well acquainted. If not, what they all had in common was that they were each looking for the Messiah. These early disciples of Jesus were diligent students of the Scripture. And they took their read-ing seriously. When the law and the prophets spoke about a com-ing Messiah, they began looking for him—and found him!

Andrew and John, as disciples of John the Baptist, were part of the whole movement that was getting people ready for the Mes-siah. When the day finally came that the Baptist pointed out the Lamb of God, they immediately followed Jesus because they had been anticipating his arrival (v. 36). The text says, "they followed Jesus" (v. 37). This indicates a commitment to discipleship; Andrew and John were serious followers. They wanted to stay with Jesus and have fellowship with him in private; so they followed him to where he was staying. John even recalls the exact time (the "tenth hour," which is about 4 P.M.) he first stayed with Jesus, much like many believers recall the time they first received Jesus. It was a special time for John and Andrew—a time never to be forgotten. From this time forward, these two men followed Jesus in the most adventurous and significant journey of all time. They had become the first followers of Jesus Christ.

Andrew knew that his brother, Simon, was also looking for the Messiah. This is implicit in the way Andrew says to him, "We have found the Messiah" (v. 41). Evidently, Peter also had been looking for the Messiah, and quite possibly had also been with John the Baptist—or at least heard him preach. When Andrew brought

Simon to Jesus, the Lord changed Simon's name to "Cephas," which is the Aramaic word for "stone." This was a prophetic name-change because Peter would become a keystone in the building of Christ's church (Matt. 16:16–18; 1 Pet. 2:4–5). Throughout his days with Jesus it appears that Simon was anything but a stone, but after Christ's resurrection and Pentecost, Simon was strengthened and fortified. Much would have to happen to Peter to bring about a transformation of his character, so as to make him a pillar and a foundation stone in the building of the first-century church (Gal. 2:9; Eph. 2:20). Peter had a way marked out for him from the very beginning—a way that conformed him to the image of his Master.

The Second Day of the Journey (1:43–51)

Most likely, Andrew and Peter told Jesus about Philip, who was from their hometown, Bethsaida. He, too, had been expecting the coming of the Messiah. This is implicit in his statement later to Nathanael, "We have found him" (v. 45). When Jesus went to Bethsaida and called Philip to follow him, he did so immediately. Then Philip went to get Nathanael. Earlier, Andrew had found Peter (his brother) and brought him to Jesus. Philip now does the same with Nathanael, who is called Bartholomew in the Synoptic Gospels.[3]

Philip told Nathanael, "We have found him who Moses wrote about in the law, and about whom the prophets also wrote—Jesus of Nazareth." This statement shows that Philip was one who read the Old Testament Scriptures and was looking for the predicted Messiah. Moses had written about him in the law (Deut. 18:15–18), and the prophets had foretold his coming. The prophets, however, never said that he would come from Nazareth, though Isaiah had predicted that a great light would arise out of Galilee (Isa. 9:1–2).[4] Nathanael, who also knew the Scriptures, took exception to the idea that the Messiah could come from Nazareth. Philip did not try to argue with Nathanael; instead, he brought him to Jesus.

When Jesus saw Nathanael coming, Jesus said, "Here is a true Israelite, in whom there is nothing false." Jesus could see into Nathanael's inner character; he saw that he was void of deceit, cunning, and falsehood; in short, he was guileless.[5] That wasn't all Jesus could see. According to his prescience, Jesus had seen Nathanael sitting under a fig tree before Philip talked to him (1:48).

According to Jewish tradition, the expression "to sit under the fig tree" could have been a euphemism for meditating on the Scriptures. But according to a literal reading of the text, it means that Nathanael was actually sitting under a fig tree. If this is understood euphemistically, it means that Jesus saw Nathanael reading the Scriptures; if taken literally, it means that Jesus had the power to describe exactly what Nathanael was doing before Philip talked to him. Such knowledge—of both his inner character and outward activities—overwhelmed Nathanael. He immediately recognized that Jesus was "the Son of God and the King of Israel."[6] This declaration shows that Nathanael ascribed to Jesus two messianic titles: one showing his divinity ("the Son of God"; Ps. 2:7), and the other showing his royalty ("the King of Israel"; Ps. 2:6; cf. Zeph. 3:15).[7]

To Nathanael and the four other disciples gathered around him—all of whom were euphoric in their realization that they had found the Messiah—Jesus said, "You will see greater things than that. . . . You will see heaven open, and the angels of God ascending and descending on the Son of Man" (1:50–51). As students of the Old Testament, his disciples would have realized that he was alluding to Jacob's vision of the ladder connecting heaven to earth (see Gen. 28:10–15). To a true Israelite, Jesus revealed himself as the fulfillment of Jacob's (who became Israel) dream. He had come to make this dream a reality, and now Nathanael and the other disciples would see the Son of Man[8] as the One who connected heaven to earth and earth to heaven. Furthermore, Jesus was the true Jacob, the true Israel—the spiritual leader of God's new tribe of men (not the twelve sons of Jacob, but the twelve disciples). Just as God had appointed Jacob to be the father of the twelve tribes (under the new name, Israel), God had appointed Jesus to be the founder of the new spiritual kingdom.

This chapter is charged with the excitement of anticipation and discovery. The Baptist has pointed to the long-awaited Messiah, and a handful of seeking young men are the first to find him. These men, who are about to begin the most dramatic journey in human history, must have been ecstatic. Their eyes were the first to see the Messiah, the King of Israel, and they were the first to recognize him as God's Son.

This excitement reaches a crescendo in the last verse. Jesus will not disappoint these men—he will reveal to them even greater things! When he says, "You will see the heavens opened," it is as if to say "Nothing about me will be hidden from you." They would fully see that the man among them was the glory of heaven and the link between the heavens and the earth. If they stayed with him, they would receive a full revelation of Jesus' identity. He was the new Israel who had come to build the new Bethel, God's house; and the disciples—whether they knew it or not—would be foundation stones in that building. Their revelation of Jesus qualified them as the keystones of God's building. Foreseeing all this, Jesus had renamed one of them "Cephas," *petros* (a stone). Peter, typical of all the other disciples, would be a significant stone in Christ's building.

In conclusion, it should be pointed out that Jesus' messianic identity is wonderfully unveiled in this chapter. Few portions of Scripture are so heavily packed with christological titles. He is called the Christ (v. 41; cf. Ps. 2:2; Dan. 9:25), the Son of God (vv. 34, 49; cf. 2 Sam. 7:12–14; Ps. 2:7), Lord (v. 23; cf. Isa. 6:1), the Lamb of God (vv. 29, 36; cf. Isa. 53), the one Moses wrote about (v. 45; cf. Deut. 18:18), the one the prophets wrote about (v. 45; cf. Luke 24:44), the King of Israel (v. 49; cf. Ps. 2:6; Zeph. 3:15), and the Son of man (v. 51; cf. Dan. 7:13). One of the reasons these declarations may appear so soon in the narrative is that John wanted to make it clear that the disciples were drawn to follow Jesus because he was immediately revealed to them as the Messiah-God. However, it would take many years for these revelations to become clear, immovable impressions in their minds.

The Third Day in the Journey: A Wedding in Cana of Galilee (2:1–11)

The excitement of the previous days must have carried over into the next days, when Jesus and his disciples were invited to a wedding celebration in Cana of Galilee. A wedding symbolizes a new beginning; it has the promise of fresh unfoldings and procreation. Indeed, a wedding is supposed to be the best of all human experiences, bringing fullness and complete satisfaction. The festivities are a celebration of this new adventure in life. But this celebration was dying out because the wine was running out—a picture of the human condition. The marriage has the promise of a new beginning, but love and the love of life will run out just like the wine runs out. Jesus had come to change this situation. With him, the wine does not run out—life does not lose its verve and vitality.

The wedding was also a picture used by the prophets and Jesus to signal the advent of the messianic age, when God as the bridegroom would join his people, the bride, in eternal, blissful matrimony (see Isa. 61:3–11; 62:1–12; Matt. 25:1–13). This wedding is pictured as an endless celebration in the Book of Revelation, wherein God's people are forever supplied by the river of life and tree of life, and are forever blessed with the face-to-face presence of God himself.

This small wedding in Cana of Galilee was a picture of that celebration to come. Not only did Jesus grace this wedding with his divine presence; he uplifted an ordinary—even failing—celebration into one that was extraordinary and extremely satisfying, and he did so by changing ordinary water into the best wine. Although the guests at the festivities did not know how this change took place, the disciples (who must have been watching Jesus' every move) knew. They were witnesses of Jesus' revealed glory.

In biblical times some wedding festivities lasted as long as a week. While Jesus was attending this wedding celebration, the wine ran out. Mary urged him to do something about this lack—just what she hoped he would do is not stated. It was then that Jesus told his mother, "My hour has not yet come" (2:4). Elsewhere in this Gospel, all statements about Jesus' "hour" refer to the time of Jesus' glorification through death and resurrection (7:30, 39; 12:23–24; 17:1). Jesus was living for that hour; it marked the culmination of his journey. After his death and resurrection, he would be fully glorified, and all men would or, should, know that he is the Son of God. But until that time, he would prove his identity by signs and miracles, even though he would rather have people believe in him without having to perform signs (see comments on 2:23–25).

In this passage Jesus must have been referring to the same hour. If so, he was, in effect, saying to his mother, "I know they have no wine, and I know that I should supply that wine to them—even that I myself should become that wine to them, but I cannot really do so until I am crucified and resurrected. Then, I will give them the best wine." So instead of providing them with the spiritual wine, he would, at that time, give them a miraculously made wine—but a temporal one. In so doing, Jesus provided them a sign as a pre-figurement of that coming glory. That sign was a manifestation of his glory, and his disciples believed in him. Thus, in taking care of the temporal problem he displayed his eternal glory.

The scene that John portrays is, in a sense, an acted-out parable (as in 13:1–17), whereby Jesus gives a preview of the glorious transformation power that will become available after his own glorification through death and resurrection. Then, what is symbolic, the water changed to wine, will become real—ordinary lives will be changed for the better. G. H. C. MacGregor says, "It is an axiom of our Gospel that the transformation of the symbolical into the 'real' can only come about with the bestowal of the Spirit, which in turn cannot take place till after Jesus' death."[9] Throughout this Gospel, one symbol after another is presented—wine, water, bread, river, light, vine—to depict the gift of life Jesus came to bestow on those who believe and receive him. But none of the symbols could become realities until Jesus was glorified and the Spirit of Jesus was imparted into the believers. Nonetheless, this miracle shows that Jesus came to give fullness of life to the human experience.

Symbolically, the miracle shows how Christ had come to fill an empty religion (symbolized by the vessels used for religious purification) with spiritual reality (symbolized by the best wine). This is a recurrent motif in John's Gospel: Jesus had come to give spiritual substance to a hollow religion.

The Beginning of His Ministry: Capernaum (2:12)

Capernaum, which was about fifteen miles west of Cana and which lay on the western shore of the Sea of Galilee, became Jesus' base of operation throughout his ministry. He, with his family, made a home there (Matt. 4:13)—to which he would retreat at various times throughout his three-year ministry (Mark 2:1; 9:33; John 4:46; 6:59). Jesus performed his second sign by healing the son of a Gentile official who came from Capernaum (see 4:46).

3

Revealing the New Temple and Kingdom

John 2:12–3:36

The disciples now begin the first leg of the journey; they go with Jesus to Jerusalem for the first Passover since Jesus' baptism. The disciples were probably shocked to see how Jesus treated the established religious leaders in Jerusalem and the revered Jerusalem temple. Instead of affirming them, he declares their need for purification and regeneration. They need a new temple, and they need a new birth. But it is only by believing in Jesus as the Son of God that they can enter the new temple (the risen Christ), and it is only by regeneration that they can enter the kingdom of God. Those who experience this would become his loved ones—the bride of the heavenly bridegroom.

Jesus, the Temple of God (2:13–22)

In this passage, the temple in Jerusalem is used to reveal Jesus as God's dwelling place. The temple that Jesus entered was the one rebuilt by the returned remnant (see Ezra and Nehemiah) and enlarged by Herod. It was God's temple, "my Father's house," as Jesus called it. But the Jews had turned it into an emporium, a place for merchandising. The Jews had become involved in the business of religion. They made a good profit on selling animals to be offered for sacrifice, and it was convenient for the people not to have to bring their animals all the way to Jerusalem. Such activity was indicative of the time preceding the destruction of the first temple and the subsequent Babylonian captivity. Due to the Jews' neglect of God, God had abandoned them; his glory had left the temple (see Ezek. 10).

Standing in contrast to the physical temple in Jerusalem was Jesus, the new and true dwelling place of God. Through the incarnation, God had taken up his abode in him. In the prologue John said, "the Word was God . . . and the Word became flesh and tabernacled among us, and we gazed upon his glory" (1:1, 14). The Son of God had come to dwell among men as a man named Jesus. He was God "tabernacling" (pitching his tent) among men. The shekinah glory of God had taken up a new residence. Without the Jews realizing it, a new age with a new temple had come into being. The worship of God would no longer be in Jerusalem or in its temple (4:20–24). God had acquired a new temple—Jesus. This was intimated at the end of chapter one, when Jesus pointed out that he was the fulfillment of Jacob's dream. Because Jacob saw heaven and earth connected, he called the place of his vision "Bethel," meaning "the house of God." Thus, Jesus—in pointing to Jacob's vision—was indicating that he was the antitype of Jacob's ladder and also of Jacob's "Bethel."

Standing in the midst of the Jews was God's house full of God's shekinah glory. The glory was no longer in the physical temple; the glory was in Jesus. But the glory was hidden from them because it was veiled within Jesus' humanity. A day was coming, however, when that glory would be released in full expression—that would be the day of Christ's resurrection, the day in which the Son of man would be glorified. Thus, Jesus' resurrection was the one sign that would prove he was the Son of God (Rom. 1:3–4). The Jews would destroy this temple, but in three days he would raise it up. The resurrected Christ would be God's new dwelling place for all the true worshipers.

John had his reasons for positioning Jesus' cleansing of the temple at this point in the narrative, rather than at the end of Jesus' ministry, as in the Synoptic Gospels (see Matt. 21:10–17; Mark 11:15–19; Luke 19:45–46). John wanted to show that Jesus knew from the beginning that the Jewish temple could no longer be considered the house of God. God was not honored there and was not living there. The temple was as empty of his presence as were the hearts of the religious leaders. Had God's presence been welcomed among them, they would have recognized and gladly received God's Son. But they had filled the temple with religious profiteering, and they would reject and even destroy the one who came to them with God's presence. In place of this temple, Jesus would build a new spiritual temple. This rebuilding would begin in the final hour of his journey, wherein crucifixion would lead to resurrection and the new construction of the church, the body of Christ.

Jesus' resurrection was the unique sign that he was, in fact, the Son of God, the habitation of God's glory. As believers in this new age we no longer need to worship God in a physical place; we worship God in spirit and in his Son. God's Son is our sanctuary (*naos* in Greek—the word Jesus used in 2:19, 21, in reference to himself),[1] our Holy of Holies. We take refuge in him, we worship in him, and we abide in him. When John saw the New Jerusalem, he said that he did not see any temple *(naos)* in it, "for the Lord God the Almighty and Lamb are the temple thereof" (Rev. 21:22).

When the disciples watched Jesus cleanse the temple, they (who had some knowledge of the Scriptures) may have had some understanding of his actions. This messianic purging of the temple was predicted in Malachi 3:1–4 and Zechariah 14:21; Jesus' proclamation, "zeal for your house will consume me," came from Psalm 69:9. The disciples, however, would not have immediately understood what Jesus meant when he said, "Destroy this temple and in three days I will build it up."[2] But after Jesus rose again from the dead, "they believed the Scripture, and the word which Jesus had said" (2:22). Many of Jesus' statements were enigmatic to the disciples until after his resurrection. After he arose, their eyes were opened to understand the Old Testament Scriptures that foretold his resurrection (see Ps. 2:7 quoted by Paul in Acts 13:33 and Ps. 16:9–10 quoted by both Peter and Paul in Acts 2:24–32 and 13:35–37, respectively).

The Regeneration of a Nation (2:23–3:21)

While Jesus was in Jerusalem during the Passover celebration, he must have performed many miraculous signs (2:23). As a result, the people believed in him. But they believed him to be a miracle-worker or a great teacher, not necessarily the Christ or the Son of God. In short, they believed in him when and only when he performed miracles. Jesus knew this because he knew human nature. Consequently, he did not trust their trust (or, belief) in him.[3]

Nicodemus was no different from any other man. He, like most men, believed in Jesus only as a miracle-worker or great teacher, but did not really believe in Jesus as the Messiah and Son of God. Jesus, knowing all men, knew this about Nicodemus from the outset.[4] Indeed, Jesus treated him as a typical man in need of divine regeneration in order to enter the spiritual realities of God's kingdom. In this light, Nicodemus was the archetype of all Israel, who desperately needed spiritual regeneration.

When Jesus told Nicodemus, "You must be born again," he was not speaking to Nicodemus alone. In the Greek text the word for "you" is plural. Nicodemus had come to Jesus as if he (Nicodemus) were representing Israel, for he spoke to Jesus on their behalf (see 3:2, where Nicodemus said "we know"). In turn, Jesus spoke to Nicodemus as Israel's representative; what he said to Nicodemus applied to all Israel (see 3:6, 11–12, where Jesus said, "you all must be born again," "you all do not receive our testimony," and "how . . . will you all believe?"). Israel needed a corporate regeneration to become part of God's spiritual kingdom.

The corporateness of the regeneration, hidden in English translations, is clear in the Greek text of 3:6. In this verse, the neuter *to* could possibly designate "the nation" or "the people." This would yield the translation, "the people born of the flesh are flesh, and the people born of the spirit are Spirit." Lest we think the last clause is impossible, 3:8 provides a metaphor comparing the wind/spirit *(pneuma)* with the person born of the Spirit *(pneuma).*

Jesus first told Nicodemus that regeneration was necessary before a person can see (i.e., understand) the kingdom of God (3:3). Then Jesus said that a person must be born of water and Spirit to enter into the kingdom of God (3:5). This statement has perplexed commentators since the day it was written. Some have said that the water indicates physical birth and the Spirit, spiritual birth. Others have said that the water signifies baptism and the Spirit, spiritual birth. Others think the water signifies the "water of the Word" (see Eph. 5:26) or the "washing of regeneration" (see Titus 3:5) that accompanies the spiritual rebirth.

From my study of the Gospel of John it would seem that the first view is unlikely, the second possible, and the third most probable.

According to the Greek, the new birth is said to be "*of* water and Spirit" (one experience with two aspects, as is designated by one preposition governing both nouns), not "born *of* water and *of* Spirit" (which would indicate two experiences). As such, the "water" signifies the cleansing and life-imparting action of the Spirit. This is substantiated by John 7:37–39, where the Spirit is likened to flowing waters, and by Ezekiel 36:25–27, where the cleansing and regenerating of Israel are associated.

After making these two statements about the new birth, Jesus used two illustrations from the Old Testament to help describe the new birth. The first illustration came from Ezekiel 36–37. Of course, this is not readily apparent. But Jesus had expected Nicodemus, the teacher of Israel, to have known what he was talking about when he likened the new-birth experience to Spirit generating spirit and to the *pneuma* blowing where it wills. Ezekiel 36 records God's plan to give Israel a spiritual regeneration, and Ezekiel 37 depicts the corporate regeneration and revitalization of Israel. As was emphasized before, Jesus was speaking to Nicodemus as if he (Nicodemus) were Israel's representative. All of Israel needed to be born again. All of Israel needed the words spoken by the Lord to Ezekiel:

> A new heart also will I give to you,
> and a new spirit will I put within you;
> and I will take away the stony heart
> out of your flesh, and I will give you
> a heart of flesh.
> And I will put my Spirit within you,
> and cause you to walk in my statutes,
> and ye shall keep mine ordinances, and
> do them. (Ezek. 36:26–27, ASV)

In Ezekiel 37 we read about the wind, the breath, and the Spirit as if they were one entity. Indeed, all three elements are translated *pneuma* in the Septuagint (so also in John 3:6–8). The *pneuma* is Spirit, the *pneuma* is breath, and the *pneuma* is wind. This *pneuma,* which regenerated the dry bones, would regenerate Israel and indeed all the world (see 3:16), if they believed.

Nicodemus did not understand the things Jesus was talking about. So Jesus turned to another Old Testament Scripture—one very familiar to Nicodemus—to illustrate people's need for regeneration. Jesus referred to Numbers 21:6–9 by comparing his being lifted up on the cross to Moses' lifting up the serpent on the pole. The children of Israel had sinned against God, so God sent fiery serpents to bite them. The venom killed many people and would have killed more had not God offered a remedy to the repentant Israelites crying out for mercy. God told Moses to make a serpent of brass and set it on a pole. Anyone bitten by a serpent could live, if he or she looked upon the brass serpent on the pole. In like manner, Christ would be lifted up on the cross in the likeness of sinful flesh, yet without sin (Rom. 8:3; 2 Cor. 5:21), to give life to all who would believe in him.

All humankind, due to their sin and rebellion, has been bitten by the sting of death. But God has provided a vicarious sacrifice: he sent his only Son to die on the cross in our stead. Whoever believes in him will not perish but have eternal life. Numbers 21:8 declares "look and live"; John 3:15 proclaims "believe and have life." Christ's vicarious death has become the unique source of life. The rest of the verses in this pericope (vv. 16–21) underscore this truth.

John the Baptist Extols Jesus, the Bridegroom (3:22–36)

At this point in the chronology of Jesus' ministry, John the Baptist is near the end of his own journey, for the time is just prior to his imprisonment (see 3:24). Therefore, this account gives John the Baptist's final words. In them we see the spirit of a man who was perfectly clear about his mission. John's journey was to prepare the way for Jesus' journey. John was not the way, the truth, or the life; but he knew that Jesus was and he was bold in his declaration about him.

John, the evangelist, opens this section with a scene in Aenon near Salim in the land of Judea. Jesus and his disciples resorted there and they began to baptize. John the Baptist was also there baptizing. Two baptisms were going on at the same time in the same place, and people were coming to one or the other. This scene was not so pleasant; it possessed an air of competition. Verse 24 heightens this tension with the foreboding word, "For John was not yet put into prison." Then the same verse exposes that there was a striving between the disciples of John and a Jew over purification.

The first four verses of this pericope reveal that there was competition. But the problem was not with John the Baptist himself; the problem was with his disciples. They were jealous that Jesus' disciples were also baptizing (for Jesus himself did not baptize but his disciples—4:2) and that many people were following him. And their striving with a Jew over the matter of purification may have added to their agitation, for one can infer that the questioning may have had something to do with whose baptism really purified. John's? Or Jesus'?

Having such jealousy in their hearts, they approached John and said to him, "Rabbi, he who was with you beyond Jordan, of whom you have testified, behold he baptizes and all men are coming to him" (3:26). These disciples of John, like many young, immature Christians, were full of a competitive spirit. They approached their leader probably expecting that he was of the same disposition. But John was not as they; his heart was pure. His response to them, which was a real test as to where he stood, revealed a transparent character. He had no motive for self-gain, no spirit of competition. The problem was in his disciples' hearts, not his.

We must be careful not to blame John the Baptist. If we had been there, we might have told him, "John, it is your fault that your disciples are like this. You should have commanded them to follow the Lamb of God. You prepared his way, and now you are in his way. Stop baptizing and send all your disciples to him." In a sense, this reprimand would have been correct because even God may have moved John out of the way by allowing him to be put into prison. I do not believe, though, that this was done as a discipline to John, but rather John was sacrificed for the sake of his disciples and for all the seekers of God. God would not tolerate any competition with his only Son; and since John's ministry had done just that, John had to be removed from the scene. However, John himself was pure, as is revealed by his testimony concerning Christ in the following verses (27–36).

John's reply to his disciples was the response of a spiritual man, a man who knew his place in God's plan. He knew that a man is not able to do anything unless it has been given to him from heaven (v. 27). Therefore, it would be foolish for John to strive against the heavenly will. If everyone was going to Christ, then everyone *should* go to Christ. John repeated to his disciples what he already announced: "I am not Christ, but I am he who has been sent before him" (v. 28). He had been forthright with all his disciples in declaring that Jesus was the Christ and that he was not the Christ. Some of his disciples (Andrew and John) had heard his announcement and followed Christ (see 1:35–40). Undoubtedly, any of his disciples could do the same, but John could not command them. They needed a revelation to follow the Christ—for no one could come to him unless the Father had drawn them (6:44).

John recognized that Jesus was the Bridegroom, that the bride belonged to him. Christ was the attractive One, the charming One, the lovely One, to whom all God's people, as his bride, should be attracted. John pictured himself as being the bridegroom's friend, or, as we would say in modern parlance, "the best man." As the best man, John enjoyed being with his friend, the bridegroom; he did not expect to be receiving any attention. All the attention should go to the bridegroom and not the friend of the bridegroom. In the Old Testament, God was likened to a bridegroom and his people to a bride (Isa. 62:5; Jer. 3; Ezek. 16; Hos. 2). In saying that Jesus was the bridegroom, John was implying that Jesus was the divine husband of God's people; as such, all of God's people belonged to him—or, as John said it, all of the increase belonged to him.

According to the following verses (3:31–36), John the Baptist gave further witness to Christ's supremacy and preeminence. First, John compared himself to Jesus. Jesus, as the "One who came from above, was over all, but John, as one who came from the earth, was of the earth and spoke of the earth. John recognized the validity of Christ's testimony, a testimony that was rejected by most but certified by a few. After this witness, John exalted the Son's special position with the Father and unique function on earth. Jesus was the One sent by God, the One loved by the Father, and the One given everything by the Father. Jesus was the One speaking the words of God and giving forth the immeasurable Spirit."[5]

4 Following the Savior of the World

John 4:1–54

This chapter is strategically placed because it follows those chapters that reveal Jesus' mission to bring into being a new, spiritual temple and kingdom—both of which transcend Jerusalem and Israel. In fact, Jesus leaves Jerusalem and Judah to go to Samaria and Galilee in search of people to participate in this spiritual kingdom. As such, an atmosphere of inclusiveness pervades this chapter. Samaritans and a Gentile receive the gospel, and Jerusalem is denounced as the place where God is found and God is to be worshiped. God is Spirit, Jesus declares; he is everywhere, and can be worshiped by anyone, whether Jew or Gentile, if they worship him in spirit and in reality.

In a sense, this chapter anticipates Revelation 21 and 22, where we see God providing the rivers of water of life to all the believers and where the Lamb and God are the temple in the New Jerusalem. The believers receive life from God and they worship in God. There is a profound, even mystical connection between drinking of the Spirit and worshiping God in the Spirit (see 1 Cor. 12:13). This is also described in Ezekiel 47, which pictures the river flowing from God's temple as a symbol of God's never-ending supply. In John 4 Jesus provides the living waters to all who receive the gift of God, and he directs people to a new temple, a spiritual one, where God is worshiped in spirit.

As provincial Galileans, the disciples must have been amazed to see Jesus approach a Samaritan woman and then bring the gospel to an entire Samaritan village. Following this, he pronounced a cure for the son of a Gentile official. These actions provided an object lesson for his apostles in the future. For they, too, would go beyond Jerusalem to bring the gospel to the Samaritans and Gentiles. John and Peter were responsible for going to the first Samaritan believers after Pentecost and providing the way for them to receive the baptism of the Holy Spirit (Acts 8:14–17). And Peter was the first apostle to bring the gospel to the Gentiles (Acts 10).

Jesus, the Messiah for the Samaritans (4:1–42)

Jesus had to pass through Samaria on his way to Galilee. Samaria was a region between Judea and Galilee in which a people of mixed blood (half Jewish and half Assyrian) dwelt. During the Babylonian and Assyrian captivities, the Assyrians left many weaker Israelites in the Israeli territory of Samaria and simultaneously forced many Assyrians to move into Samaria, all of which led to intermarriage and the progeneration of a mixed race. The Jews hated them. In fact, when the remnant returned from Babylon they refused the Samaritans any partnership in rebuilding the temple and Jerusalem, even though the Samaritans claimed that their God was the same as the Jews' (see Ezra 4:1–6 where they are called "adversaries"). The Samaritans had adopted the Pentateuch as their Scriptures and set up a place for worship on Mount Gerizim in accordance with Deuteronomy 11:26–29; 27:1–8, but they were far from having an accurate knowledge of the truth, although they knew about the Messiah.

After a long journey, Jesus was tired. So he sat on a nearby well. This well was on a piece of land that Jacob had given to his son, Joseph (see Gen. 33:19; 48:22; Josh. 24:32). After Jesus had met the Samaritan woman, she mentioned that Jacob gave them (the Samaritans) this well. In short, the well was a precious gift that had been handed down from generation to generation. Jacob, his sons, his cattle, and generations since had drunk from the well. No doubt, the Samaritans greatly prized it. But Jesus had a better gift to offer: "the gift of God" (4:10).

That well could never satisfy, but the gift of God would bring eternal life. The Samaritan woman treasured a corruptible gift, but Jesus offered her an eternal gift. The water from Jacob's well could never satisfy, but the water that Jesus would give her would become a fountain in her springing up into eternal life, a fountain always supplying her with the fresh, divine life.

As far as the woman was concerned, it required work to fetch the water from this well. In fact, in verses 11–12 she called it a cistern (*threar* in Greek). But Jesus considered the well to be a fountain (*pēgē* in Greek).[1] Since the water in a cistern lies stagnant at the bottom, it is hard to fetch; but the water in a fountain spontaneously springs up. Jesus offered the fountain of life. Whoever drinks of the water that he gives will have an inward fountain of water springing up into eternal life.

Of course, the woman wanted this living water, but some self-realization and honest confession were needed first. When the Lord summed up her life story, she acknowledged that he must be a prophet, and then launched off into a discussion concerning the religious debate between the Jews and the Samaritans over which place of worship was the right one—Jerusalem or Mount Gerizim. The Samaritans had set up a place for worship on Mount Gerizim in accordance with Deuteronomy 11:26–29 and 27:1–8; while the Jews had followed David and Solomon in making Jerusalem the center of worship. The Scriptures affirmed Jerusalem as the true center for worship (Deut. 12:5; 2 Chron. 6:6; 7:12; Ps. 78:67–68). But Jesus told her that a new age had come in which the issue no longer concerned a physical site. The Father would no longer be worshiped in either place. They, the Samaritans, worshiped that which they did not understand. The Samaritans had some notion of God, but the Jews knew the God of the Old Testament. Furthermore, salvation came from the Jews (not from the Samaritans), for the Savior himself sprang from among the Jews. But even though the Jews were far superior to the Samaritans, a new age had come in which the true worshipers (Jew, Samaritan, or Gentile) must worship the Father in spirit and in truth.

"In spirit" corresponds to Jerusalem, and "in truth" corresponds to the Samaritans' unknowledgeable ideas of worship, God, and the like. Formerly, God was worshiped in Jerusalem, but now the true Jerusalem would be in a person's spirit. Indeed, the church is called "the habitation of God in spirit" (Eph. 2:22). True worship required a people to contact God, the Spirit, in their spirit, as well as a people who knew the truth. New Testament worship must be in spirit and in truth. Since "God is Spirit," he must be worshiped in spirit. Human beings possess a human spirit, the nature of which corresponds to God's nature, which is Spirit. Therefore, people can have fellowship with God and worship God in the same sphere that God exists in.

Following the Lord's discussion with the Samaritan woman, she was convinced that he was the Messiah. She joyfully proclaimed this in her village. In the meantime, Jesus' disciples returned with the food they had bought. But Jesus told them that he had eaten another kind of food—that is, he had been satisfied by doing the Father's will. That was his food. And to see the Samaritan woman recognize him as the Messiah was more satisfying than drinking from the well of Jacob. Jesus realized that the Samaritans were ripe for the harvest; they were ready, like sheaves of wheat, to be brought into the experience of obtaining eternal life—just like grain is brought into the granary.[2] The harvest was white because others had labored; now the disciples should be ready to reap because of others' labor. Indeed, after the church began, the gospel went to the Samaritans—and there was a great harvest (see Acts 1:8; 8:1; 9:31; 15:3). Even at that time, many in the Samaritan village of Sychar believed that Jesus was the Messiah.

In Jesus' encounter with the Samaritan woman and with the Samaritans in Sychar, he reveals that he is "the gift of God" (4:10), who gives the fountain of the water of life to each believer (v. 14). He also reveals that he is the expected Messiah (vv. 25–26). As a result, the Samaritans believed that Jesus was "the Savior of the world." This declaration is the climax of this passage concerning Jesus with the Samaritans, for it speaks of how Jesus had come not just to be the Jews' Messiah but the world's Savior, even of those despised by the Jews.

Jesus, Healer of the Gentiles (4:43–54)

Recall some of the first verses of this chapter (vv. 3–4). Jesus was leaving Judea to go to Galilee, and he had to pass through Samaria on the way. After a two-day stay in Samaria, he went on to Galilee. Verse 44 explains why he went there: "For Jesus himself testified, a prophet has no honor in his own country." Because Jesus knew that a prophet receives no honor in his own country

(Judea), he purposely left there for Galilee. Jesus' native "country" was Judea; thus, Jesus departed there because he was not really received in Judea and went to Galilee where he knew he would be received. The strength of this interpretation comes from verse 45, which says that the Galileans welcomed Jesus.[3]

When he was in Galilee, he was approached by an official from Capernaum, who asked Jesus to heal his son. Assuming this passage is parallel to Matthew 8:5–13 and Luke 7:1–10,[4] it can be inferred that the official was a Roman centurion. If so, this is the first and only instance in John's Gospel where Jesus has contact with a Gentile. (Of course, this excludes his exchange with Pilate during his trial.) As such, we have a chapter that presents Jesus giving the gift of life to the Samaritans and then to Gentiles. With the Samaritans, the woman at the well first believes and then many in Sychar do (v. 39). With the Gentiles, the official believes and then his household does (v. 53). In both instances, the people believe Jesus' word (v. 41 and v. 50) and thereby receive life.

The presentation of the gospel first to the Jews (chap. 3) and then to the Samaritans and Gentiles (chap. 4) is a precursor to the pattern displayed in Acts. The disciples' first missionary journey would follow the journey Jesus took. They began in Jerusalem, went out to Samaria, and then beyond to the Gentiles (see Acts 1:8; 8; 10). And they, too, preached the word of life, which was received by all who believed the good news.

5 Hearing the Life-Giver and Judge

John 5:1–47

This chapter advances the journey motif because it affirms chapter 4 by emphasizing Jesus' plan to bring life and light to the whole world, not just to the Jewish nation. In this chapter Jesus claims that he has the power to give eternal life to all who believe in him, and he has the power to execute judgment over every human being in the eschaton. He heals a paralyzed man to demonstrate his life-giving powers, but this action causes the Jewish leaders to judge him for working on the Sabbath.

Sooner or later a conflict would erupt between Jesus and the established religious leaders in Jerusalem. In the Synoptic Gospels this conflict is deferred until the end of Jesus' journey; in John the conflict is immediately put in the forefront by (1) the contrast between Moses as the law-giver and Jesus as the grace-giver in the prologue, (2) the placement of the temple cleansing in Jerusalem as early as chapter 2, and (3) Jesus' confrontation with the Jerusalemite leaders here in chapter 5.

Some writers have thought the Gospels were written as apologies for Jesus' life and ministry, much the same as Plato's *Socrates*. Indeed, Jesus is on trial throughout this Gospel. It's as if John wants Jesus to answer every charge against him and every question about him. This is nowhere more apparent than in John 5, wherein Jesus' divine identity and messianic mission are questioned and incontrovertibly affirmed. The irony of this situation is that Jesus, while on trial, affirms that he is the judge of all.

Jesus Heals on the Sabbath (5:1–18)

Although John does not specifically mention the name of the festival Jesus attended in Jerusalem, there is good reason to believe it was Pentecost.[1] During the intertestamental period the Jews used Pentecost to celebrate the giving of the law through Moses on Mount Sinai (Jubilees 1:1; 6:17). Furthermore, the Jews observed the ordinance that they should not do any servile work during Pentecost (Lev. 23:21). For Jesus to heal a man on the Sabbath and then command him to walk around with his mat constituted a double breach of the law according to the Jews. But Jesus was giving mercy to a man who had been paralyzed for thirty-eight years, a man who was weary of existence and running out of hope.

It is possible that the thirty-eight years are symbolic of the period of time Israel was in the wilderness (see Deut. 2:14), experiencing the harsh effects of sin. If so, this emphasizes the sick condition of Israel—a nation paralyzed with sin, hoping superstitiously for angelic intervention to revive them. What they really needed was a divine infusion of life from the Son of God. Jesus made this proclamation to Nicodemus, and here demonstrates his life-giving power on a child of Israel. But the religious leaders failed to see anything significant or wonderful about this miracle. Blinded by their fervency for the law, the Jewish leaders considered Jesus a rebel against the Mosaic law and Moses himself. Ironically, Moses was actually one of Jesus' chief advocates (5:45–46).

Jesus on Trial (5:19–47)

After the Jews discovered that Jesus had healed the invalid on a Sabbath day, they confronted Jesus as to what authority he possessed for violating the Sabbath. Jesus told them that he was working in cooperation with his Father. This incensed the Jews even more. They realized that in his calling God "My Father" (v. 17) Jesus was saying, "I am God's Son, equal to God." For Jesus to say that God was his very own Father was to make himself equal to the very God (v. 19). This was unthinkable to the Jews. In fact, this was blasphemy. From that day forward the Jews sought to kill him.

One of the reasons Jesus' statement was unthinkable to the Jews was that they had not considered the Messiah to be divine. To their way of thinking, the Messiah would come from the loins of David.

He would be a man—a wonderful man indeed, but still a man. They had no thought that the Messiah would or could be God. The thought that God would become man startled the Jewish mentality. Jesus did not attempt to explain this mystery to the Jews. Instead, he tried to tell them how, according to his works, he demonstrated his oneness with God, the Father. Jesus indicated that he was not able to do anything by his own initiative. There was no possibility for him to act independent of the Father. He only did that which he saw his Father doing. All of his works testified of his union with the Father and dependence on him. These works would increase in greatness as a testimony to the Jews.[2]

These works would show the Jews that Jesus was indeed the Messiah. Jesus preferred that the people would believe in him for his person, but he would also accept their faith if they believed in him on account of his works (see 14:11). In the rest of the verses (21–30), Jesus describes how he and the Father work together in raising the dead, imparting life, and executing judgment. Jesus, as the Son of man, was given the authority to execute judgment and to give life. These are his two primary functions. He gives life now, to those who are spiritually dead, by means of his life-giving word; and he will give life later to those physically dead, awaiting the resurrection.[3] Those who have believed him will participate in the resurrection that gives eternal life, but those who have not believed will participate in a resurrection that brings about their judgment and eventual condemnation. In all of this work, the goal is that people would honor the Son as they honor the Father.

Jesus concluded his defense by providing the Jews with a five-fold testimony. They had questioned his authority and assaulted his identity. In response, Jesus indicated that he had five very reliable witnesses: (1) the Father himself (5:31–32, 37), (2) John, the Baptist (vv. 33–35), (3) his works (v. 36), (4) the Scriptures (vv. 39–40), and (5) Moses (vv. 45–47). According to the Jewish law, truth or validity has to be established by two or three witnesses (Deut. 17:7; 19:15). Therefore, Jesus' self-witness would not validate his claims; he needed the witness of another. That other witness was not John the Baptist, but his Father. In the following verses, Jesus called upon several witnesses to affirm his claims, but actually he needed only one witness, his Father's.

In any event, Jesus had five witnesses to defend his claims, and all these witnesses were accessible to the Jews. They had heard John the Baptist, that burning and shining lamp, who pointed the way to the Light.[4] They had seen the miraculous works of Jesus. They also had the Father's testimony—had they been receptive to him (see 8:47). They researched the Scriptures daily, thinking they could gain eternal life by this endeavor.[5] And they searched the Scriptures for statements about the coming Messiah. The Scriptures attested to the kind of Messiah Jesus was, but the Jews were too focused on the kind of Messiah that was yet to be. Jesus came as the suffering Lamb; they were looking for a conquering King. Nevertheless, the Scriptures abound with testimony to him. And Moses himself wrote of him (see Deut. 18:15–18).

The Jewish leaders criticizing Jesus did not have God's word residing in their hearts. If that word had been abiding in their hearts (see 8:31; 15:7), they would have recognized the One to whom the Scriptures give testimony (see 5:39). They had the greatest of all God's manifestations standing right before their eyes—Jesus, the Word, the visible expression of God to men. But the Jews would not come to him that they might have life.

6 Giving Manna from Heaven

John 6:1–71

T his chapter signals a turning point in the spiritual journey presented in this Gospel. As in the exodus pilgrimage, there is a definite call for the new sojourners to keep on following the Lord. Some do, but most don't. Those who choose to keep on following Jesus—and there are only eleven of them by the time this chapter concludes—are the true Joshuas and Calebs. The rest of Jesus' followers quit the journey.

This chapter is heavily dosed with exodus imagery. Even the setting reflects the exodus. It is Passover (the second one recorded in John). As the Passover is the commemoration of the Jews' exodus from Egypt under the leadership of Moses and a celebration of God's wonderful provision to his people (from the day they left Egypt to the day they entered Canaan), so Jesus is presented as the true Moses, inviting the people to follow him, and as the true manna come down from heaven to give life to the world.[1] To provide this bread would cost Jesus his life. The sacrifice of his life, like the breaking of bread before it was multiplied, would give life to the world. This would be the ultimate act in Jesus' journey.

Mingling imagery of bread and sacrificial lamb, Jesus presents himself as the one who must die in order for others to live. To receive his life one must accept his death. But this message was veiled in harsh language: "Unless you eat me you have no life in you." All but the Twelve were offended by Jesus' words, and many of his other disciples no longer journeyed with him (6:66). This marks the critical turning point in the spiritual journey. Only the Twelve realize that Jesus has the words of life and choose to continue with them.

The Multiplication of the Loaves (6:1–15)

The multiplication of the loaves is the only miracle (besides Christ's resurrection) recorded in all four Gospels. All four writers must have been impressed with the miraculousness of the event. John specifically used the event to prepare the way for Christ presenting himself as the bread of life. John often used a physical setting or actual event to provide a platform for presenting some spiritual reality of Christ. The temple in Jerusalem served as a good backdrop for Christ to be presented as the real sanctuary of God, and the well in Samaria was an excellent figure of Christ as the fountain of living waters. The multiplication of five barley loaves and two fish into a munificent feast was a picture of how Jesus, through death and resurrection, would feed the world with his abundant life.

Seeing this miracle caused the people to believe that Jesus was "the Prophet" Moses had predicted (Deut. 18:15–18). And since Moses was a prophet who (in their opinion) fed the children of Israel in the wilderness (see comments on 6:31–32), so Jesus must have been the Prophet predicted by Moses, who was now feeding them in the wilderness.

They were not wrong to think of Jesus as being the Moses-like, Moses-predicted Prophet, because he was; but they were mistaken to think he was a military deliverer. And he would have nothing to do with them when they wanted to force him to be their king. The people wanted someone to lead the Jews in rebellion against Rome in order to gain freedom for Israel. The people expected this of the coming Messiah and of the coming Prophet (it was not clear to the Jews that one person would be both). When Jesus realized their intentions, he departed.

Crossing the Sea of Galilee (6:16–21)

As Jesus was alone on a mountain, the disciples boarded a boat and started to cross the sea. When a storm arose, the disciples were in grave danger. But Jesus, walking on the sea to them, rescued them. There is not as much detail about this miracle in John's Gospel as in the Synoptic Gospels probably because the incident is not central to chapter 6. John wants to get his readers from the multiplication of the loaves to the discourse on the bread of life, for this is the central theme of John 6. Besides, his readers would have known of this famous incident on the sea; so he gives it in brief.

Nevertheless, the account does have a place in John 6 and accords quite well with the journey motif of the Gospel. The journey of the disciples on the sea is a precursor to the spiritual journey they will experience in the future. As such, the whole story can be read symbolically. Jesus alone on the mountain could depict his heavenly, divine position. Out on the sea, separated from Jesus, the disciples encounter darkness, followed by great winds and waves. This could represent their earthly lives and concomitant struggles. Through all of this, "Jesus still did not come to them." They were left alone to struggle for "three or four miles" against the wind and waves. Finally, Jesus comes to them as the "I am," the divine provider, and swiftly takes them to shore—the goal of their journey.

Jesus, the Bread of Life (6:22–59)

The multitude who had eaten of the loaves found Jesus on the other side of the sea. They were seeking him because he had satisfied their appetites, not because they had seen a sign (v. 26). To those caught in the drudgery of sustaining life Jesus said, "Stop laboring for the perishing food but labor for the food that remains to eternal life" (v. 27). This was Jesus' introduction to his great and profound discourse on the bread of life.

Jesus told the people that the food they were striving and working for would not give them eternal life. But if they believed in him (which was the work of God), they would have eternal life. The people would not believe in him, however, until they saw a sign. After all, their ancestors ate manna in the wilderness for forty years— whereas Jesus had just fed them for one day. They even quoted the Scriptures to Jesus: "He gave them bread from heaven to eat" (v. 31, from Pss. 78:24; 105:40). But Jesus told them, "Moses has not given you the bread from heaven, but My Father is giving you the true bread from heaven. For the bread of God is he who comes down from heaven and keeps on giving life to the world" (6:32–33).[2] Just as the manna came down every day to supply the sojourning Israelites, the Lord, as the real manna, comes down and continually gives life to the world. The manna that had been given to the Israelites in the wilderness had no present effect on the Jews of Jesus' day. Their boast in the ancient miracle could not give them life. Jesus was the real bread of God, who came to be the ever-present manna, the ever-present life-giving supply.

They, of course, wanted this bread. But when Jesus kept telling them that he himself was the bread of life, even the bread that came down from heaven, they became more and more offended. How could Jesus, a mere man, be the bread of God? How could Jesus, the son of Joseph and Mary—people the Jews knew—come from heaven?[3] The offense increased even more when Jesus told the people that he had come to give his flesh for the life of the world (i.e., he had come to sacrifice his life so that the world could have eternal life [v. 51]). He demanded that people eat his flesh and drink his blood. If they didn't, they would have no life in them. This was repulsive to the Jews. They were commanded by the law not to drink blood (Lev. 3:17; 7:26–27; 17:10–14). But Jesus' death—the shedding of blood—enables people to have eternal life. To eat his flesh and drink his blood is to appropriate, by faith, the meaning of Jesus' death. The blood separate from the flesh evidences a death—and what a glorious death, a death that has enabled millions to receive the eternal life.

Before Jesus, the bread of life, could be eaten by anyone, he had to die. This is conveyed in the words, "the bread I will give for the life of the world is my flesh." The Greek word *huper* (meaning "on behalf of"—also translated as a benefactive "for" in English) is used by John and other New Testament writers with respect to Jesus' death to signify his substitutionary, benefactive death on the cross (see 10:11, 15; 11:50, 52). To give of his flesh meant Jesus gave over his body to death on the cross, so that by his death the world (i.e., humanity) could have life. This was the ultimate step in his journey—the one most costly to him but most advantageous to the world. His death provided bread for the world.

Throughout the discourse Jesus kept urging his listeners to feed on his flesh and drink his blood in order to have eternal life, to dwell in God and be indwelt by him, to live by Jesus, and to live forever. The Jews, and even most of his followers, were astounded and incredulous. Jesus knew that this was a difficult concept to grasp. So, he told the people that no one could come to him unless the Father had drawn him. No one would believe in him unless they had been among those whom the Father had given to Jesus (see 6:37–40).[4] All believers belonging to that corporate group would never be cast out. Instead, they would receive eternal life as a guarantee that they would participate in the resurrection of life. How blessed to be among those chosen by the Father to be drawn to Jesus and to believe in him. To all such believers, he is the bread of life.

A Turning Point in the Journey (6:60–71)

Many of Jesus' disciples[5] were so offended at his words spoken in the Capernaum synagogue that they decided not to follow him anymore. It seems that they were especially offended to have heard a man declare that he had descended from heaven (6:62). If so, then these followers had never realized Jesus' divine identity. To these who lacked this revelation, the words of Jesus probably sounded like those of a madman and a raving lunatic. Imagine hearing someone tell you that he had come from heaven and that you must eat him in order to live forever. You would think he was insane or divine.

The Twelve remained with him because they had come to realize that Jesus was divine. When Jesus asked them if they, too, wanted to leave, Peter (speaking for all of them) declared, "Lord, to whom shall we go? You have words of eternal life. We have believed and have known that you are the Holy One of God."[6] This declaration, which parallels the one Peter made at Caesarea Philippi, is strategically placed, for it affirms the disciples' resolve to continue on the journey with Jesus.

To these faithful followers, Jesus gave the key to interpreting his previous message: "The Spirit is the life-giver, the flesh profits nothing; the words I have just spoken to you are spirit and life." Jesus had not been asking the people to eat his physical flesh—"the flesh profits nothing." The people needed to understand that Jesus could not be appropriated until he had become life-giving spirit (1 Cor. 15:45) and/or until the Spirit would come to make his message vivified in the believers' experience.

In the next chapter, John plainly tells us that no one could really drink of Jesus until the Spirit of the glorified Jesus became available. In like manner, no one could really eat Jesus until the Spirit was available. However, people could receive spirit and life through the words of Jesus. His very utterances ministered spirit and life to the believers. In this regard, the people in Jesus' day could then and there receive spirit and life (see 3:34 and note, and 5:25). But Jesus could not be eaten or drunk (as it were) until the Spirit became available via his resurrection. Now, in this age, we can partake of Jesus as the bread of life and water of life via the Spirit (see 1 Cor. 12:12). In Jesus' time, however, it was his word (the instant, spoken utterance—Greek *rhēma*) that ministered spirit and life to people. The twelve disciples had received this word; they could never leave him. Peter, speaking on their behalf, proclaimed, "Lord, to whom shall we go? You have words (Greek *rhēmata*) of eternal life, and we ourselves have believed and have known that You are the Holy One of God" (6:68–69).

We, in this age, are blessed to have the life-giving Spirit. He has come to us to illumine and vivify Jesus' message, and he has come to us conveying Jesus as the bread of life. Through the Spirit we can partake of Jesus, the real manna, the ever-present supply, and be continually satisfied in him.

Journeying with the Smitten Rock and Light of Life

John 7:1—8:12

hapter 7 is central to the journey motif inasmuch as it places the Festival of Tabernacles in the foreground of the narrative. The tabernacle was the preeminent symbol of Israel's wilderness journey, for it represented God's accompanying presence with his people as they sojourned from a land of bondage to a land of freedom. Jesus had come as the new tabernacle of God, to be with his people and to lead them from the bondage of spiritual darkness and death into the freedom of life and light in the Spirit.

During the Festival of Tabernacles, the Jewish people commemorated God's provision (of water) for his people in the wilderness and presence among them (in the pillar of fire) by pouring out water on a rock and by lighting lamps. Jesus here presents himself as the true fulfillment of the smitten rock (providing spiritual nourishment for the journey) and the light of life (illuminating those walking in darkness).

At this juncture in John's narrative, he also begins to concentrate on the manifold sufferings Jesus encountered during his ministry. From the end of chapter 6 through chapter 7 and following, we see a suffering Jesus—one constantly pierced with the jabs of unbelief and hostile slander. It is in the midst of this suffering that one figure emerges: the smitten Rock. The more the Rock was smitten, the more he gave life-giving water. It was no accident that on the last day, the great day of the Festival of Tabernacles, Jesus stood and cried, "If anyone thirsts, let him come to me and drink." Jesus' wounds became the founts of blessing.

Jesus Rejected (7:1–36)

Near the end of John 6 we saw how most of Jesus' disciples abandoned him—that is, all but the Twelve. And among the Twelve, there was a betrayer, Judas Iscariot, who was in league with the devil. At the beginning of John 7, we learn that Jesus had to leave Judea and go to Galilee because the Jews were seeking to kill him. So Jesus remained in Galilee for quite a while, for the most part staying in his own home. It is hard to imagine that Jesus would have taken such a long respite from his ministry. Jesus' brothers couldn't believe it either, so they urged him to manifest himself to the world, if indeed he were the Christ. His own brothers didn't believe he was the Messiah, but they urged him to go to the Feast of Tabernacles. Jesus declined, but then later went in hiding.

At the festival, the crowd was looking for him. And while they were looking and waiting, they all began to express their opinions. Some said he was a good man; others thought he was a deceiver. Some wondered how he knew the Scriptures if he did not have formal training in Jewish literature.[1] Others thought he was demon-possessed. Others were convinced that Jesus, a Galilean and a son of Joseph and Mary, could not have been the Messiah because no one was supposed to know where the Messiah came from. In the midst of all this din, Jesus cried out, "You both know me and know where I come from. Indeed, I have not come from myself, but he who sent me is true, whom you do not know. As for myself, I know him because I am from him and he sent me" (vv. 28–29).

Jesus' mission would not last long because he was about to return to the Father who sent him. But the journey back to the Father would have to go through Calvary. Jesus said, "I am with you for a short time, and then I am going away to the one who sent me" (v. 33). Aware that the Jewish religious leaders were seeking to kill him, Jesus here alludes to his coming death (see 8:21–22). This statement indicates that no one would be taking Jesus' life from him; rather, he would depart this life according to the preordained time and then return to his Father.

The Jews, not understanding that Jesus' statement referred to his departure via death, wondered if he was speaking about going where the Jews were scattered among the Greeks (called "the dispersion" or "the diaspora")—where he would also teach the Greeks. The Jews listening to Jesus wondered if he was about to depart Judea and go to these Jews to teach them and the Greeks among whom they lived. Jesus, of course, never went to the Greeks (see comments on 12:20–24), but his Spirit through the church brought the gospel to the Greeks. At the time John wrote his Gospel, many Greek churches existed—most notably, the one in Ephesus, the church John served in his later years. Thus, there is irony in the question the Jews asked, for little would they have imagined that the gospel of Christ would go to the Greeks.

Jesus, the Smitten Rock (7:37–52)

The climax of this passage comes "on the last and greatest day of the festival." This would be the eighth day, the culmination of the festive occasion. During the Festival of Tabernacles, the Jews celebrated the memory of how God had tabernacled with their forefathers in their sojourning, guiding them on their way and providing them with manna and water from the smitten rock. Every day during this festival (except the last one) a priest, standing in front of the temple, would take a golden pitcher of water and pour it on a rock, in commemoration of the water flowing out of the smitten rock (see Exod. 17:6). While the water flowed out, the people standing by would chant, "Therefore with joy shall you draw water out of the wells of salvation" (Isa. 12:3). A priest would also read Zechariah 14:8 on the first day of this festival: "And it shall come to pass in that day that living waters shall go out from Jerusalem."

These promises of living water were wonderful, yet they were merely promises. No one could really take a drink; consequently, the people were still thirsty. Thus, Jesus stood and shouted out, "If anyone is thirsty, let him come to me; and let him drink who believes in me. As the Scripture[2] has said, streams of living water will flow from within him." Jesus' invitation can be rendered in two ways: (1) Jesus is the source from which the living waters flow (as just translated—see also NEB, NJB, RSVmg, NIVmg); (2) the believer is the one from whom the living waters flow, as in the following translation: "Jesus stood and cried out, 'If any man thirsts, let him come to me and drink. He who believes in me, as the Scripture said, will have rivers of living water flowing from his innermost being.'" In the second rendering, the word "his" before "innermost being" refers to the believer; in the first, "his" refers to "Jesus." The first rendering seems more suitable, for it is Jesus who is the antitype of the smitten rock, not the believer.

Jesus would become the true smitten Rock by being crucified on the cross and giving forth the life-giving water. Even prior to his crucifixion he suffered the blows of persecution, insult, and unbelief. He did not retreat or withdraw in the face of suffering; rather, he took the smiting as a chance to let the living waters flow and give life to others.

After Jesus' declaration, John added an explanatory note: "And this he said concerning the Spirit whom those who believed in him were about to receive; for the Spirit was not yet because Jesus was not yet glorified" (7:39). This explanatory note, in context, has nothing to do with whether or not the Spirit yet existed. Of course, the Spirit existed; but the Spirit about to be made available through the glorification of Jesus was not yet.[3] In short, the Spirit of the glorified Jesus was not yet available for the believers to partake of. One could not actually come to Jesus and drink of him until Jesus was glorified and became Spirit.

In context, this statement was part of a parenthetical explanation provided by John, a statement providing the reader with the key to understanding Jesus' declaration in verses 37–38. Jesus had just promised that anyone who believes in him could come to him and drink of him and thereby experience an inner flow of living water. John's parenthetical remark makes it clear that Jesus was promising the believer an experience of the Spirit that could not happen until after Jesus was glorified and the Spirit was made available. John's word does not mean that the Spirit did not exist at the time Jesus spoke (cf. 1:33) or that believers had not received the spirit and life of Jesus' words (see 6:63, 68). John's note pointed to a time when the Spirit of the glorified Jesus would become available through a special dispensation to all who had believed in him. Thus, the availability of the Spirit is linked with the glorification of Jesus, for it was after Jesus' glorification via death and resurrection that the Spirit became available to the believers (see 20:22).

In other words, once Christ became life-giving spirit through res-urrection (see 1 Cor. 15:45; cf. 2 Cor. 3:17–18), he could be received as living water.

Remember, Jesus had said, "If anyone thirsts let him come to me and drink." If Christ as spirit was to become drinkable, something had to happen to him so that he could be drunk. He had to become Spirit so that he could be appropriated (cf. 1 Cor. 12:12). Glorifi-cation would be the means through which Jesus would be "pneu-mafied." According to the Gospel of John, Jesus' glorification would be achieved through the process of death and resurrection. John 12:23–24 indicates that Jesus likened his glorification to a grain of wheat falling into the ground, dying, and then bringing forth much fruit. Through this process a single grain would be transformed into a stalk of wheat. Paul expanded upon the same illustration in 1 Corinthians 15 and explained how the body is transfigured through death and resurrection. During the course of his expla-nation, Paul indicated that Jesus, as the last Adam, in resurrection had become "life-giving spirit." He, like the grain, had been sown in corruption, dishonor, and weakness; but he was raised in incor-ruption, honor, and glory. Simultaneously, he became Spirit.

The revelation of the Lord becoming Spirit through the glorifi-cation of resurrection is progressively presented in John's Gospel. John does not tell us from the beginning that the Lord could not really give the eternal life to men until the Spirit was made avail-able through resurrection. John keeps us in suspense, awaiting "the hour" in which the Lord, passing through death, would enter into his glory. In the meanwhile, the Lord kept announcing to peo-ple their need to believe in him and receive him as the eternal life. He told Nicodemus about his need for regeneration, he announced to the Samaritan woman that she could drink the waters of life, and he offered himself as the bread of life to a multitude of Jews. Albeit, Nicodemus could not then and there be fully regenerated, the Samaritan woman could not fully drink, and the multitude could not yet eat (except to the extent that each of the people received the Lord's word as spirit and life [6:63], but such partaking would be but a foretaste of the Spirit yet to come). It was not until the Spirit would be available that the Lord could be received as the regenerating life, the water of life, and the bread of life. Neverthe-less, John is silent about this in chapters 1–5. In chapter 6, it is intimated in verse 63, because there the Lord indicated that "the Spirit is the life-giver, the flesh profits nothing." Finally in chapter 7 John spoke a plain word to inform the reader that the Lord's promise of receiving life could come only by receiving the Spirit, and that the Spirit would be available only when Jesus was glorified.

Jesus, the Light of Life (7:40–8:12)

After Jesus' profound exclamation on the final day of the Feast of Tabernacles, some believed that Jesus was the Prophet, and others even believed that he was the Christ. But still others demurred: "Does the Christ then come out of Galilee?" According to the traditional interpretation of the Old Testament, the Jews were convinced that the Messiah must come from the seed of David and be born in Bethlehem. This was based accurately on many verses (2 Sam. 7:12–16; Pss. 89:3–4; 132:11; Isa. 9:6–7; 11:1, Mic. 5:2). Jesus was indeed the Son of David, born in Bethlehem, but due to his early flight to Egypt and return to settle in Galilee, he was known throughout his lifetime as a Galilean. The Pharisees held the same view as the crowd did about the origin of the Messiah. When Nicodemus tried to defend Jesus, they retorted, "Are you also from Galilee? Search and see that a prophet is not raised up from Galilee" (7:52).

Jesus refuted their position, not by trying to prove that he had really been born in Bethlehem, but by declaring, "I am the light of the world; he who follows me shall not walk in darkness but will have the light of life" (8:12). (In the original text of John, 8:12 immediately follows 7:52. The story about the adulteress was a later addition, interrupting the true narrative.[4]) By making this declaration, Jesus was clearly alluding to Isaiah 9:1–2, which states, "Beyond the Jordan, Galilee of the Gentiles—the people that walked in darkness have seen a great light; they that dwelt in the land of the shadow of death, upon them hath the light shined" (ASV). The reader cannot but notice how similar Isaiah 9:2 and John 8:12 are. Both speak of the light shining on the people, both indicate that these people walked in darkness, and both relate light to life. The Pharisees were so confident in their knowledge of the Scriptures. They knew that the Scriptures never spoke of a prophet coming from Galilee. But the Scriptures did speak of a great light appearing to the Galileans, a great light intimately related to those people who lived in the land of the shadow of death. Jesus was that great light.

Though Jesus suffered the people's unbelief and derision, he was (and still is) their source of life and light. He is the smitten Rock, the source of living waters; he is the light of the world, the light that gives life. Suffering did not cause him to become withdrawn and resigned. Rather, the wounds opened the flowing fountain. What a constant source of life he is!

Presenting the I AM

John 8:12–59

A t this point in the journey, the disciples have heard many of Jesus' self-pronouncements, and they have come to recognize that he is Christ, the Son of God. They must have also begun to realize that he was the spiritual reality of all that Israel revered and adored ceremonially. Unfortunately, the Jews were holding an empty shell. Jesus was the egg and yolk, but they—repulsed by him—refused to eat. Still, Jesus presented himself as the bread of life to be eaten and the water of life to be drunk. He is what we all need for the spiritual journey. He is the "I AM."

This is exactly how God had revealed himself to Moses and the children of Israel before calling them on their exodus out of Egypt (see Exod. 3:1–18). In presenting himself as the "I AM," God was saying, "I am all that you need for the beginning of your journey, the continuance of your journey, and the conclusion of your journey." From start to finish, Yahweh, the I AM WHO I AM, was the full provider. When Jesus presented himself as the "I AM," he was simultaneously affirming his divine identity and presenting himself as the divine provider for the spiritual journey. But most of the Jews—especially the Jewish leaders—rejected his claim to divinity and thereby forfeited his never-ending, all-sufficient supply. As a result, they never took the first step in following Jesus; they didn't go on the journey. They affirmed their allegiance to a bygone leader, Moses, but they wouldn't follow the new pioneer, Jesus, because they questioned his identity.

Jesus, the I AM (8:12–59)

No other portion of John, even of the entire Bible, is so focused on the controversy over Jesus' identity as John 7 and 8. The Pharisees were relentless in their query: Who are you? Who are you? Who are you? They had to know if Jesus was claiming to be the Messiah. But Jesus would not come right out and tell them, "I am the Messiah." He told the Samaritan woman, but he wouldn't tell these querying Jews, although they desperately wanted him to do so (see 10:24). Although Jesus wouldn't tell them directly, he revealed his divine identity in many ways—all through a series of "I am" statements. There are eight such statements in John 8, each of which contains another unveiling of his person: (1) "I am the light of the world" (v. 12), (2) "I am not alone" (v. 16), (3) "I am he who testifies" (v. 18), (4) "I am from above" (v. 23), (5) "I am not of this world" (v. 23), (6) "I am he" (vv. 24, 28), (7) "I am principally that which I also speak" (v. 25), and (8) "I AM" (v. 58).

I am the light of the world. Jesus declared "I am the light of the world" to the Pharisees who never thought that a prophet, much less the Messiah, could ever come from Galilee (see 7:41–42, 52).[1] True, the Scriptures never spoke of the Messiah or a prophet in relationship to Galilee, but the Old Testament certainly spoke of a great light coming to the people of Galilee: "beyond the Jordan, Galilee of the Gentiles. The people that walked in darkness have seen a great light; they that dwelt in the land of the shadow of death, upon them hath the light shined" (Isa. 9:1–2, ASV). Christ was the great light that had come to shine on all people, both Jew and Gentile. Christ was the light *of the world.* And this light brought life to those who walked in darkness and dwelt in the land of the shadow of death. It is amazing how parallel Isaiah 9:2 and John 8:12 are to each other. Surely, those Pharisees who knew the Scriptures so well should have realized that Jesus was alluding to Isaiah, but they were blinded by their unbelief.

I am not alone. Due to their blindness, the Pharisees did not perceive who was in their midst; they thought Jesus was a mere man. Nor did they realize that Jesus had come from God the Father and was still accompanied by God the Father. Jesus was not alone; the Father who sent him came with him. Jesus twice asserted this: "he who sent me is with me" (8:16, 29). Jesus had not come on his own, and Jesus did not do anything on his own initiative (see vv. 28, 42). He was completely dependent on the Father. He spoke only what he heard from his Father, and he taught only that which he had seen together with the Father (see vv. 28, 38). In short, he lived by the Father and to please his Father (vv. 28–29). But the Pharisees did not know Jesus as God's Son because they did not know God the Father, although they claimed to. Actually, Jesus told them that their father was the devil because they, like the devil, would be murderers (vv. 41–44). They claimed Abraham as their father and even God as their Father, but their intended evil actions exposed another source—not Abraham, not God, but the devil, who was a murderer from the beginning.

I am from above . . . I am not of this world. It must have startled the Pharisees to hear Jesus say that he was from above, even that he was not of this world. He was either crazy or divine. By contrast, Jesus told the Pharisees that they were from below and were from this world. His origin was heavenly and divine; their origin was satanic and worldly. The two were in completely different realms. Jesus, coming from his realm, entered into theirs—the light came into the realm of darkness—but they did not comprehend him.

I am he (or, *I am the One* or, *I am who I am*). Earlier it was said that Jesus did not come right out and tell the Jews, "I am the Christ." But he came very close to making this pronouncement. In 8:24 he said, "for if you do not believe that I am he, you will die in your sins." According to the Greek, Jesus simply said "If you do not believe that I am." The subject after the predicate nominative must be supplied. Here, and in 8:28, Jesus was telling the Pharisees that they would die in their sins if they did not believe he was who he was. In declaring "I am he" or "I am the One" or "I am who I am," Jesus was revealing that he was the Christ that they had been looking for. But if they did not believe this, they would die in their sins.

They didn't believe this. So, in their unbelief they had Jesus crucified. Nevertheless, Jesus predicted that "when you lift up [i.e., crucify] the Son of Man, then you will recognize that I am he" (8:28). The Lord's crucifixion would bring about a universal knowledge of his identity. After his crucifixion and subsequent glorification through resurrection, Jesus would be recognized as the Messiah by Jews and Gentiles alike.

I am principally that which I also speak.[2] When the Pharisees pressed Jesus to declare his identity, he told them, "I am what I say I am—my words present who I am." The Lord did not need to give them any further explanations; he had already, through his previous speeches, again and again unveiled his identity to them. In short, the Word revealed himself through his words. But the Pharisees were not able to understand his speech because they were deaf to his word (8:43). Had they been of God (i.e., ones belonging to God) they would have heard the special utterances (Greek *rhē-mata*) of God. Jesus had revealed the truth through his words, but the Pharisees were not receptive.

There were some Jews, however, who did believe in him. Jesus told them that they should remain in his word, for by so doing they would know the truth that would set them free (vv. 31–32). He even told them that they who keep his word would never taste death (v. 52). Both these promises offended the unbelieving Jews. They thought they were free because they were the sons of Abraham, but actually they were in bondage to sin.[3] And they knew that all people—including their beloved Abraham and the prophets—had tasted death. How could Jesus promise freedom *and* immortality? Who was this Jesus that he could make such bold promises?

Before Abraham came into existence, I AM. The Jews had boasted of their association with Abraham, but Abraham had rejoiced to see the day of Christ's coming.[4] But how could Jesus and Abraham have seen each other, the Jews queried? Jesus wasn't even fifty years old. Then Jesus startled the Jews with the bold declaration, "Before Abraham came into existence, I AM." In one breath, he asserted his eternal preexistence and his absolute deity. Abraham, like all mortals, came into existence at one point in time. But Jesus, unlike all mortals, never had a beginning. He was eternal. And he was God; for by declaring I AM, he was stating that he was the ever-existing, self-existent God, the I AM WHO I AM (see Exod. 3:6). Offended by his claim to deity, the Jews took up stones to stone him, but he escaped.

Jesus left Jerusalem behind, abandoning the beloved city to its own spiritual ruin (cf. Matt. 23:37–39; Luke 13:34–35). He would return one last time, but only to be crucified. From here on, Jesus parted ways with the Jewish establishment in Jerusalem. Subsequently, his task was to call his believers out from Judaism, even as a shepherd calls his sheep to leave the fold for lush, green pastures. In the following chapters, we will see this Shepherd on the move.

9 Leading God's People from Darkness to Light

John 9:1–10:21

t this point in the journey, Jesus is about to desert Jerusalem and forsake Judaism, but he can't forget his mission. He had been sent by the Father to call out his sheep from Judaism's fold and lead them into the green pastures of abundant life. God had sent him to give light to those in darkness and to give life to those in a lifeless religion. The enlightened and enlivened ones would become the sheep in Jesus' new flock, composed of Jewish and Gentile believers.

In this section Jesus is revealed as God's sent one: he was sent like the stream to Siloam to give the water of life; he was sent like rays from the sun to give light to the blind on earth; and he was sent like a Shepherd to gather God's sheep from among the Jews and Gentiles.

The man born blind typifies the condition of everyone on earth. We are born into darkness, and we are born into judgment. We need salvation from this darkness and from judgment. In this story the man born blind is enlightened both physically and spiritually—in contrast to the religious leaders who are incurably blind.

The sheep symbolize the true followers of Jesus, the Messiah-Shepherd. Jesus had come to take them from the fold of Judaism, where they had been kept in waiting for their Shepherd. While held there, they were harassed by thieves and wolves, but their care-takers (the religious leaders) didn't guard them from danger. Unlike the Shepherd who loved his sheep and would give his life for them, the religious leaders were selfish cowards.

Jesus, the Sent One and the Light of the World (9:1–41)

John often used a physical object to depict a certain spiritual reality of Christ's person. John used Jacob's well to show Christ as the fountain of living water, and the manna to illustrate Christ as the bread of life, and the smitten rock at the Feast of Tabernacles to show Christ as the source of living waters. Here, in John 9, John uses the pool of Siloam to depict Christ as the sent One (for John makes a point of telling us that Siloam means "sent"). This symbolism ties in nicely with the declaration Jesus made at the beginning of chapter 9: "We must work the works of him who sent me, while it is still day. Night is coming when no one can work. While I am in the world, I am the light of the world" (vv. 4–5). Christ was sent by God to be the light of the world.

But it is also important to note that Jesus here includes the disciples, for he was speaking of himself and his disciples as co-workers when he said, "We must work the works of him who sent me."[1] The disciples were to learn from him because they would continue his work as his sent ones (see 20:21). He included the disciples in this work (although they did nothing for this blind man) because they would continue to shine forth his light after Jesus' departure (see Phil. 2:15). Those following Jesus in this journey would themselves become the sent-ones (lit. the apostles).

The healing of the blind man was a powerful display of Jesus' deity. In all the Old Testament there is no record of a blind man being healed (see 9:32), but it was predicted that the Messiah would heal the blind (Isa. 29:18; 35:5; 42:7). For Jesus to cure a man born blind set him apart from all human beings, even the greatest of the prophets. The way in which he performed the healing—as odd as it may seem—sparkled with divinity. The act of spitting on the ground and forming clay from the dirt is reminiscent of the way in which God created man (see Gen. 2:7). From antiquity, spit or saliva was thought to have medicinal power. Jesus' saliva had creative powers (cf. Mark 7:33; 8:23, where Jesus used his saliva to cure a deaf and dumb man in Decapolis and to heal a blind man in Bethsaida).

Another unusual aspect of this miracle is that Jesus sent the blind man, eyes covered with mud, to wash himself in the pool of Siloam. This action, however, was a display of the man's obedience to Christ's command. Furthermore, it was symbolic because "Siloam" is a Greek translation of the Hebrew name *Shiloah,* which means "sent" (9:7). The water in Siloam got there by being sent into the pool through a channel from the Spring of Gihon in the Kidron Valley. It was said in Isaiah 8:6 that the Jews refused the waters of Shiloah, just as in this chapter the Jews refused Jesus. But the blind man obeyed the word of the sent One. He washed in the water of Siloam and received his sight. These waters symbolized the work that Jesus, the sent One, had come to do. Like the cleansing waters of Siloam, he had been sent into the world to give life and light.

Another prevalent image in this chapter is Jesus as the light. Jesus was sent into this world to be its light. The man born blind exemplified the dark condition of humankind. We are inherently blind: it is our nascent condition. Blindness does not come as a particular punishment for specific sin; blindness (i.e., spiritual darkness) is the condition of fallen man. In fact, the Scriptures equate fallen humankind with darkness (see Eph. 4:18–19). This judgment and curse were already upon humankind when Jesus came (see 3:21). That is why Jesus told his disciples that neither the blind man nor his parents were directly responsible for his condition. His particular ailment exemplified the condition of all.

Jesus came into this world to give it light. Those who received the light brought glory to God; those who rejected the light had the judgment of God still remaining on them. The blind man had his physical sight restored and then his spiritual sight. He saw twice. First he saw the physical world and then he saw the light of the world. The first "seeing" came instantaneously; the second was more gradual.

The more the Pharisees questioned the man who received his sight, the clearer he became about Jesus. Their blind obstinacy augmented his clarity. The man first realized that Jesus was a prophet (9:17). Then he defended Jesus as being a man without sin, a worshiper of God, a doer of God's will, a performer of a miracle never done before, and a man from God (vv. 31–32). After he was ousted from the synagogue, he met Jesus eye to eye. Then the man, prompted by Jesus, believed him to be the Messiah and Lord.[2]

To be ousted from the synagogue was tantamount to excommunication.[3] According to Jewish regulations, there were two kinds of excommunication: one that would last for thirty days until the offender was reconciled, and one that was a permanent "ban" accompanied by a curse. Many Jews in John's day had been "de-synagogued" because they confessed Jesus to be the Christ. (This was predicted by Jesus in 16:2.) An ancient document called the Cairo Genizah (ca. 80–90) contains a curse against the Nazarenes, banning them from participating in the synagogue. In Jesus' day there was also a kind of informal prohibition against any Jew who would confess Jesus to be the Christ.

For Jesus to ask the formerly blind man to believe in him as "the Son of Man" was to request confession of Jesus as the Messiah.[4] If the man made this confession, he would be cut off from Judaism (see 9:22). This underscores Jesus' present move (at this point in the narrative journey) to abandon Judaism and take with him all who would follow. The blind man who received his sight, therefore, is symbolic of all who would desert Judaism to follow Jesus.

In contrast to the man who had received his double sight, the Pharisees had sight but no light. They were spiritually blind, though they thought they were enlightened. This was presumptuous. They assumed they knew all about the Messiah, but their knowledge blinded them from seeing the very Christ who stood in their midst. Because they thought they saw, they were blind. Those who admitted they were blind could receive the light and see, but those who thought they saw would remain in their darkness (9:39–41).

Jesus, the Messiah-Shepherd (10:1–21)

This section is directly tied with the previous chapter. In fact, 10:1–21 is a continuation of the dialogue between Jesus and the religious leaders begun in 9:40–41. The thematic link between the two chapters is that the new believer expelled from Judaism for believing in Jesus as the Messiah becomes typical of all those believers who would come out of Judaism to follow Jesus as sheep following their shepherd.

   The allegory or similitude that Jesus presents in 10:1–6 (and following) is spoken directly to the Jewish leaders. (Of course, the disciples are included in the audience.) In this allegory Jesus presents himself as the true shepherd come to call his sheep out of Judaism into a new flock having good pasture (which is the abundant life provided by the Son of God through his death and resurrection).

   An allegory is different from a parable. In an allegory each item has a corresponding significance; in a parable all the items produce one total meaning—hence, each item in a parable may not have an equivalent signification. Most of the elements in this allegory can be readily assigned a corresponding antitype:

   the good shepherd = Jesus Christ
   the sheep = the Jewish believers in Jesus
   the other sheep = the Gentile believers
   the sheepfold = Judaism
   the gate = the office of the Messiah
   the gatekeeper = God
   the pasture = the abundant life
   the wolf = destroyer of God's people (perhaps Satan)
   the hired hand = a selfish religious leader

It is difficult, however, to identify unequivocally the "strangers" and "thieves." My hypothesis is that the "strangers" are the same as "the hired hands"; they are the religious leaders who really didn't care for the sheep and therefore never earned their allegiance. The "thieves" are probably false messiahs. The Greek word *lēstēs* was used of revolutionaries in Jesus' day.[5] The Messiah was supposed to be a revolutionary leader, according to popular opinion. Many such revolutionaries came pretending (or hoping) to be Israel's Messiah (see 10:7). But all who came as such were pretenders; the sheep never followed them.

   Jesus' similitude seems to have one allegory within the other. The larger allegory pertains to the sheep and the shepherd; the allegory within this pertains to the gate. Christ is both the gate and the shepherd. The "gate" comes first (10:1–3a) and then the "shepherd" (vv. 3b–5), each with its own interpretations—the "gate" is explained in verses 7–9, and the "shepherd" in verses 11–18.

It is easy to ascertain that the good shepherd is Christ, the sheep are the believers, the sheepfold is Judaism, and the door-keeper is God. But what is the door into the sheepfold? It would seem that the door is the "Messiahship"—the office of the Messiah. Only one person could qualify for entering into that position. Jesus was the One. Since he was the true Messiah, God the Father opened the door to him. He had the legitimate access into the sheepfold of Judaism. Anyone else who tried to enter that fold had to do so by some other means, for no one else was qualified to be the Christ.

Only Jesus was the legitimate Christ, as this Gospel time and again proves. By this allegory Jesus was claiming his right to be the Christ, because the Father opened the door only to him and the sheep knew only his voice. Within the fold of Judaism were some of God's people who had awaited the coming of their Shepherd-Messiah (see Isa. 40:1–11). When the Shepherd came, he would lead his people out to good pasture (see Ezek. 34). He would call his own sheep by name and lead them out of the fold. This was exactly what happened to the blind man in the previous chapter. (In fact, it should be noted that John 10 continues the discourse Jesus was having with the Pharisees in chapter 9, a discourse that concerned the blind man's new-found sight and the Pharisees' blindness.)

After presenting the allegory, Jesus first expanded on the meaning of "the door of the sheep" (10:7–10) and then on "the shepherd of the sheep" (vv. 11–18). As "the door of the sheep," he was the One uniquely qualified to fulfill the role of Messiah. All who ever came before him (meaning "all who ever *came* pretending to be the Christ") were actually thieves and robbers. But the sheep did not hear them—for none of them possessed the authentic voice of the Shepherd. Since Jesus was the genuine Messiah, the sheep could enter through him to find salvation, liberty, and provision. The expression "will be saved" indicates spiritual salvation and spiritual security ("will be kept safe," see NIV). The statement "will go in and go out" comes from an Old Testament expression describing the free activity of daily life, that is, the freedom to come and go as one pleases (see Deut. 28:6; Ps. 121:8; Jer. 37:4). In short, the Shepherd would provide his sheep with freedom. The language of Numbers 27:16–17 (ASV) is similar: "Let Jehovah . . .

appoint a man over the congregation, who may go out before them, and who may lead them out and bring them in; that the congregation of Jehovah be not as sheep which have no Shepherd." Jesus is just that Shepherd. He gives his people safety, liberty, and provision.

As opposed to the thief (who represents the false christ) and the hireling (who denotes the religious leader who rules God's people for self-gain), Christ is the devoted and dedicated Shepherd. The sheep were being "robbed of life" by the religious leaders. By contrast, Jesus gives the abundant, eternal life to his sheep. And he demonstrated his love in that he laid down his soul for the sheep. Four times in this passage Jesus indicated that he would lay down his life for the sheep (10:11, 15, 17, 18). Jesus was, of course, alluding to his substitutionary death, in which he would sacrifice his soul, his life (*psuchē* in Greek) so that the sheep might enjoy the abundant, divine life (*zōē* in Greek). Isaiah 53:10 says the Messiah would offer "his soul a sacrifice for sins." But Jesus also had the authority to take it up again (10:18). This process of laying down his life and taking it back up again (all on his own initiative) enabled Jesus to give his believers abundant life, a life that passed through death and entered into resurrection.

What a difference between the good Shepherd and the thief and the hireling. The thief steals, slaughters, and destroys, and the hireling depicted those Jewish leaders who took their office for self-gain. In the Old Testament these hirelings were severely reproved by God (e.g., see Ezek. 34, where "the shepherds of Israel" are rebuked for abusing their office). The leaders of Israel had not shepherded Israel properly prior to the captivity; thus, many of the Jews became like scattered sheep having no shepherd (see Ezek. 34:10–16).

The good Shepherd had come, however, to gather God's people together again and bring them into one flock (see Ezek. 34:11–14, 23). This flock would consist of Jewish believers and Gentile believers (called "other sheep . . . not from this fold"). All would be brought into one flock, with one Shepherd. According to the best manuscripts, the last part of verse 16 reads, "they shall become one flock, one shepherd." This indicates that the oneness would be between the two groups of sheep and between them and the

Shepherd. In other words, the oneness of the sheep is integrally related to their oneness with the Shepherd. The one flock composed of Jewish and Gentile sheep united by and to the Shepherd is like the one body made up of Jewish and Gentile members united by and to the head, Christ (see Eph. 2:14; 3:6).

10

Consecrating a New Habitation for God

John 10:22–42

In accordance with his writing pattern, John uses the literary technique of setting a Jewish festival or Jewish sacred object as a background against which Jesus is presented as the spiritual reality of that ceremony or physical artifact. In this instance, the backdrop is twofold: the temple in Jerusalem and the Festival of Dedication (commonly known as Hanukkah). And both images are connected because the Festival of Dedication is a commemoration of the purification of the temple from its profanation by Antiochus Epiphanes. This purification, instituted by Judas Maccabeus in 164 B.C., was a rededication and reconsecration of the temple to God. Jesus is here presented as the true Temple of God in whom the Father himself resided (10:38). Jesus, the Son of God, was the one consecrated by God and sent into the world to be his representative (vv. 35–36). But the Jewish leaders did not recognize him as such, and therefore accused him of blasphemy.

The Consecrated Son of God (10:22–39)

This episode is a continuation of 10:1–21 inasmuch as this new section reiterates and even explains Jesus' previous words concerning the Shepherd and the sheep (10:25–27). This episode is also a continuation of Jesus' stay in Jerusalem, which began with his coming to the Festival of Tabernacles in 7:14. The time-gap is about two and one-half months: from the time of the Feast of Tabernacles in October to the time of the Feast of Dedication in late December.[1]

The Feast of Dedication was not one of the official festivals prescribed by the Pentateuch. It was instituted by Judas Maccabeus in 164 B.C. to commemorate the purification of the temple from its profanation by Antiochus Epiphanes, which is called "the abominable desolation" (Dan. 9:27). For three years (167–164 B.C.), the Syrians had profaned the temple by putting the idol of Baal Shamen on the altar (1 Macc. 1:54; 2 Macc. 6:1–7). This pollution of the holy place came to an end when Judas Maccabeus drove away the Syrians, built a new altar, and rededicated the temple on the 25th day of Chislev (1 Macc. 4:41–61).

John calls the Festival of Hanukkah, *ta enkainia,* which literally means "the renewal." This is key to an interpretation posited thus far in this book that Jesus had come to provide a complete spiritual renewal for the people of God, wherein he became the spiritual reality of all that they cherished. On the top of the list of their valued possessions was the temple, but it had become polluted with religious profiteering and hollow ceremony (see commentary in Chapter 2). God had decided to start over by providing his Son as the new Temple of God.

The Greek term *ta enkainia* is the idiomatic equivalent of "the dedication" (in Hebrew, *hănukā*). In the Hebrew Bible and the LXX this phraseology was used to describe the dedication and/or consecration of the altar in the tabernacle (see Num. 7:10–11), Solomon's temple (1 Kings 8:63), and the rebuilt temple (Ezra 6:16). Brown, therefore, says that "the term is evocative of the consecration of all the houses of God in Israel's history."[2] It is in this context that Jesus affirms that he is the consecrated Son of God, the dwelling place of the Father (10:36–38). He is the culmination of all God's houses; he is the house of houses.

The Jewish leaders, however, were preoccupied with only one question about Jesus' identity: Was he or was he not the Messiah? They encircled Jesus and demanded that he give them a plain answer. He asserted that he had already told them. Of course, he did not do so with plain words. Jesus had revealed his Messiahship through a similitude because it required illumination to see that Jesus was the Messiah. Furthermore, Jesus always avoided using the term "Messiah" when speaking with the Jews because the term "Messiah" connoted a military leader (much like Judas Maccabeus had been).[3]

In any case, the Jewish leaders did not believe he was the Messiah—and would not believe even if he told them—because they were not his sheep. But there were some who had heard his voice and seen the light. They were Jesus' sheep, following their Shepherd-Messiah. Jesus knew them personally and gave them this promise: "I give them eternal life, and they will never perish. And no one can snatch them out of my hand." In this grand statement, Jesus summarizes the blessings of the gospel as presented in John: the believer in Jesus has eternal life, will not perish, and is secure in his care. Jesus assured his sheep this security on the basis that both he and the Father would keep them in their hands. The Father had given all the believers (as one corporate entity) to the Son as his gift;[4] not one of them would perish.

Then the Lord told the Jews, "I and the Father are one." Because the word in Greek for "one" is in the neuter case, this statement could mean Jesus and the Father are one (1) in activity, (2) in nature, or (3) in number. All three are defensible by the context. In the immediate context, this bold assertion indicates that the Father and Son are one in the action of keeping the believers secure. Yet this unity of action has its source in an ontological oneness—the Father and Son are one in nature and in position (the two mutually indwell each other—10:38). Furthermore, the Father and Son are numerically one in the sense that the Son's hand is not any different than the Father's. Whichever meaning the Lord intended to convey, the Jews understood that he was claiming deity for himself, because they were about to stone him for blasphemy. How could he, a mere man, make himself God?!

Jesus argued that it was not blasphemous to call himself the Son of God when, in fact, he was the One the Father consecrated and sent into the world. Furthermore, was it not true that other men had been called "gods" in the Scripture? On occasion, God had called the judges of Israel "gods," inasmuch as they were his representatives. In Psalm 82 the supreme God is said to rise in judgment against those whom he calls "gods" (Hebrew *ĕlōhîm*), because they had failed to extend just equity to the helpless and oppressed.

These "gods" were those who were the official representatives and commissioned agents of God.

If God called them "gods," why was it blasphemous for Jesus, the One consecrated by the Father and sent into the world, to say, "I am God's Son"? The Jews could not argue against this because it stands written in the irrefragable Scriptures (i.e., the Scriptures are an entire entity from which no one can remove any portion). But Jesus was greater than those men who received messages from God, for he himself was the very message from God to men. And whereas they were earthly men selected by God to represent him, the Son of God came from heaven as the consecrated one, dedicated to do God's will on earth. Jesus was therefore justified in calling himself the Son of God, equal with the Father.

The Jewish leaders had asked Jesus if he was the Messiah. In his response, Jesus went one step further; he told them he was the Son of God, coequal with the Father. Knowing that the Jews could not even imagine a man being God or God being a man, Jesus gave them this concession: "even if you do not believe me, believe the works, so that you may know and continue to know that the Father is in me and I am in the Father."[5] Jesus' miraculous deeds should have been a sign to the Jews pointing to his divine identity. If they accepted his works, they could have gone on to realize that Jesus' claim to oneness with the Father was true.

A Return to the Beginning (10:40–42)

Jesus' explanations did not change the Jews' minds; they were intent on stoning him for blasphemy. So Jesus departed Jerusalem, and crossed the Jordan eastward to the place where John first baptized. This step in Jesus' journey is symbolic. Jesus' departure signals his abandonment of Jerusalem, and his return to the site where John first baptized and subsequent good reception symbolizes a new, spiritual entity taking root among the outsiders of Judaism. Jesus went to the people who had heard John the Baptist proclaim Jesus' coming. Now they saw this Messiah face to face, and many believed in him. What they now heard and saw in Jesus confirmed in their minds the genuineness of his forerunner's proclamations. Jesus stayed with these believers until it was time, once more, to return to Jerusalem, where he would face his death.

11

Raising the Dead

John 11:1–54

ohn 11, the midpoint of this Gospel, presents the apex of the Lord's ministry of life. Up until this chapter, the Lord had presented himself as "life" to various kinds of people. He was "eternal life" to Nicodemus, "the water of life" to the Samaritan woman, the quickening life to the paralyzed man, "the bread of life" to the hungry multitude, the "rivers of living water" to the thirsty worshipers, the "light of life" to the blind man, and the "abundant life" to his sheep. Now in this chapter he is life in its ultimate expression—resurrection life—to a man in his ultimate state, death. Here, the Lord's life is shown to be really life, for resurrection life is the life that can pass through death and still remain alive. Only God's life, the eternal life, is this resurrection life.[1] For Lazarus' situation, the Lord declared, "I am the resurrection and the life. He who believes in me, even if he should die, will live" (11:25). Jesus is the antidote to the finality of life.

Lazarus' resurrection is a foreshadowing of Jesus' own imminent resurrection. Jesus himself would emerge from a carved-out tomb in the not-too-distant future. Jesus knew this as he raised Lazarus from the dead. This must have comforted Jesus because he saw God's power manifest as a preview. But it also must have troubled him because he knew that he, too, must pass through death before he could enter the gates of life.

Jesus, the Resurrection and the Life (11:1–44)

When Jesus heard of Lazarus' sickness, he knew that it would lead to death—but not to absolute death, because Lazarus' death would be the means through which the glory of God would be manifested and the Son of God glorified. Having this knowledge, the Lord purposely waited two more days, until he knew Lazarus had died. Then he went to Lazarus.

The disciples could not believe that Jesus wanted to return to Judea, where he had just recently escaped being stoned (see 10:31, 39). But the Lord, as the light of the world, still had some hours of daylight to give to this dark world. According to 11:9, Jesus knew how many more hours were left in his ministry. He was moving and working intently in the time-frame allotted to him by the Father— all in preparation for his final hour. He longed that some could still enter into "the day." His earnest desire was that more people could see the light and walk in it. Just as the beaming rays of the sun awaken a man from slumber, the light of life was going to awaken Lazarus out of his sleep; and in so doing many others would also be awakened by the light. In this "twilight hour" of his ministry on earth, some would still be given the chance to believe and to see. For this cause the Lord rejoiced over the death of Lazarus. What occasion it would give others to believe in him!

Once Jesus arrived at Bethany, he was met by Martha. Unfortunately for Martha, she was exposed as one whose previous, partial knowledge hindered her from clearly seeing the present, available Christ. She knew that Jesus could have prevented Lazarus' death but not reverse it—even though she said that God would give to Jesus whatever he would ask. But apparently this did not include any thought of Jesus' ability to raise Lazarus from the dead. When Jesus said, "Your brother will rise again," her response was doctrinal: "I know that he will rise again in the resurrection in the last day." Martha completely missed the present significance of the Lord's statement because she was thinking of an event—the eschatological resurrection. Jesus revealed that he, a person, is the resurrection and the life: "I am the resurrection and the life. He who believes in me, even if he should die, will live." Lazarus had been a believer in Jesus; therefore, even though he had died, he would live.

Every believer who has died would yet live, *and* everyone who was (and is) yet *living and believing* would certainly not die forever (see 11:26). Christ did not promise the prevention of death for the believer, but he promised the life that guarantees resurrection and eternal life. But when Jesus asked Martha if she believed this, it was again exposed that she did not apprehend the present Christ; rather, she declared what she had always thought of him.[2] And though this declaration is ever so good—"I have believed that you are the Christ, the Son of God, who comes into the world"—how much better it would have been for Martha to say, "I believe that You are the resurrection and the life."

Then Mary came. Her first statement to Jesus was the same as Martha's: "Lord, if you had been here, my brother would not have died" (cf. v. 32 with v. 21). The Lord had no response, although it was evident that he was disturbed. Jesus shed some tears and manifested his agitation. While the weeping and wailing all around him may have caused him to shed tears, the unbelief that surrounded him deeply agitated and disturbed him. The text says, "When Jesus saw her weeping, and the Jews who had come along with her also weeping, he was agitated in his spirit and troubled." The Greek word *embrimaomai* (also used in 11:38) can be rendered "indignantly angered."[3] This Greek verb is consistently used in the LXX and New Testament to express anger or agitation (see Lam. 2:6; Dan. 11:30, LXX; Matt. 9:30; Mark 1:43; 14:5). Jesus must have been angry and agitated by the mourners with their excessive sorrow, Martha's lack of understanding, Mary's faithlessness, and the general unbelief.

Jesus must have been disturbed by the complaint, "Could not this man who opened the eyes of the blind man also cause that this man should not die?" (11:37). But Jesus gave no verbal response; instead, he groaned in his spirit. Then he asked that the stone be removed. Martha protested, betraying her unbelief in the resurrection about to occur. The Lord reminded her that she would see the glory of God if she believed. Jesus realized that the Father had heard him and would answer his prayer. He uttered his thanks out loud for the sake of those standing around, that they might believe that the Father sent the Son (see 17:20). As Jesus expected (but not anyone else), Lazarus came forth in resurrection—a wonderful prefigure of what the Lord himself was about to do.

Jesus' Prophetic Death (John 11:45–54)

The purpose of the resurrection miracle was to arouse faith—and this it did, not only for Jesus' followers but for many of the

Jews who had come from Jerusalem. These new believers would go back to Jerusalem and spread the word of this miracle and thereby prepare the way for Jesus' grand reception in Jerusalem when he made his triumphal entry (see 12:9–15). Thus, John 11 is essential for providing an account of the one incident that created the great popular excitement that preceded Jesus' entry into Jerusalem. This detail is lacking in the Synoptic narratives.

Although many believed in Jesus after witnessing Lazarus' resurrection, others didn't. They went to tell the Pharisees, who in turn assembled a council to determine what should be done to Jesus. Their motive was entirely selfish and their reasoning political: "If we let him go on like this, everyone will believe in him; and the Romans will come and take away both our place and our nation." If all the Jewish populace would hail Jesus as their Messiah-King, the leaders feared that the Romans would take away their limited privileges of self-rule, as well as what the leaders called "our place"—an expression that could refer to their political position(s) or to the temple, "our holy place" (cf. Acts 6:13; 21:28), the center of their religious life. They feared that their limited autonomy would be taken away because it would appear to the Romans that Jesus had created an uprising in Israel. Forty years later, in A.D. 70, the Jews did instigate an insurgence against Rome; as a result, Jerusalem and the temple were destroyed—and the Jews were expelled from their homeland. By the time John wrote this Gospel, this had already occurred.

Caiaphas, who was high priest that year, rebuked the assembly: "You know nothing at all, nor do you realize that it is better for you that one man should die on behalf of the people than the whole nation perish." Caiaphas' words clearly indicate that he was convinced that nothing short of murdering Jesus would save the nation of Israel from Roman destruction. But the next statements (in 11:51–52), inserted by John, show that God used Caiaphas in his position as high priest to utter a prediction about the worldwide efficacy of Christ's death. And this is the irony of Caiaphas' statement that John didn't want his readers to miss: Jesus' death, intended to spare the nation of Israel from physical destruction, was actually to spare Israel from spiritual destruction.

John in typical fashion explains to his readers the meaning of Caiaphas' words: "he prophesied that Jesus was about to die for the [Jewish] nation and not only for that nation, but to gather into one the dispersed children of God." For Caiaphas, this was an unconscious prophecy. Nevertheless, his words were of great prophetic significance. His prophecy indicated that Jesus would die for (or, on behalf of—Greek *huper*) the people as a substitutionary sacrifice. But whereas Caiaphas thought this death would save Israel from destruction and dispersion at the hands of the Romans, Jesus' death actually would be for the spiritual salvation of Israel and all the world—and for the gathering together (as opposed to scattering) of all God's children, both Jews and Gentiles, whoever had come to believe in Jesus as the Messiah (see 1:12; 10:16; 17:20–26). Jesus would die *not* to save the nation from the Romans but to gather together into one all the children of God who had been scattered. By his cross he would create the one new man (see Eph. 2:14). The Jewish leaders, of course, missed the prophetic implications of Caiaphas' statement and immediately began plotting to kill him.

Aware of the plot against his life, Jesus (with his disciples) retreated to a region near the desert, to a village called Ephraim, which is probably the same as Ephron, near Bethel (see 2 Sam. 13:23; 2 Chron. 13:19). This kind of retreat from danger was frequent in Jesus' pilgrimage (see 4:1–3; 7:1; 8:59; 10:40–42). His fleeing, however, was not because he feared death, but because he was waiting for the right timing. In a few months, he would enter Jerusalem during the Passover celebration, knowing full well that the prophecies concerning his death would be fulfilled.

12 Coming into His Glory

John 11:55–12:50

This passage presents a major crisis in Jesus' pilgrimage. We see him struggling as he thought of his imminent crucifixion (12:27), and yet he knew that he must go forward with the divine plan. And so the triumphal entry at the beginning of Passover week took an unexpected turn. Jesus refused the glory of the moment for the glory that would come when he, as a grain of wheat falling into the ground to die, would produce many grains in resurrection. Jesus' "hour" to be glorified had come.

This section begins with a description of the commencement of Passover week in Jerusalem. It was a time when "many went up from the country to Jerusalem in order to purify [sanctify] themselves before the Passover." Most likely, this is the Passover that occurred in A.D. 30, the year of Jesus' death. The Jewish people were lawful in preparing themselves for the Passover (cf. Exod. 12:14–20; 13:1–9), but their thoughts were not on the Passover but on Jesus—and what would happen if he came to Jerusalem for the Passover.

From Glory to Glory (11:55–12:36)

Everyone knew that the chief priests and Pharisees wanted to arrest Jesus, and that they were to report his whereabouts if he was discovered. The scene was set for Jesus' entry into Jerusalem;

but before he would go there for his final visit he would stop by Bethany to visit his friends, Lazarus, Martha, and Mary (12:1–11).

Among those who loved him were his friends at Bethany. In a world that would not receive him, among his own people who would not own him (moreover, who were intending to kill him), how comforting it must have been for him to have a place of rest and love, a home to which he could resort. Bethany was a place of sweetness and supply (Bethany means "a house of figs"). His friends were there to receive him and serve him (Luke 10:38). Whenever Jesus came to Jerusalem he did not lodge there, but he would go to Bethany to stay with Mary, Martha, and Lazarus (see Matt. 21:17).

Six days before the Passover, Jesus came to Bethany. This would be his last visit, for Jesus was on his way to be sacrificed as the Passover Lamb at Calvary. We do not know if anyone else was truly aware of this. According to the other Gospels, as well as John's, Jesus had given his disciples plenty of warning. But his word about his death did not penetrate. Who, among his loved ones, realized that Jesus was about to die? Did his disciples, absorbed as they were with the coming glory? Did Lazarus, recently raised from the dead? Did Martha, obsessed with her serving? It seems that only Mary perceived that Jesus' death was imminent. Perhaps she realized that evening would be her last with him. This would be her final chance to demonstrate her love to him. She had been keeping a very costly, precious ointment for just such an occasion.

When supper ended, she took the spikenard, anointed the feet of Jesus, and wiped off his feet with her hair. The house was filled with the fragrance! Others were offended that Mary would waste this ointment, but Jesus pointed out that this ointment was not wasted on him. Of course, the money could have been given to the poor, but there would always be the poor. Yet they would not always have Jesus. Mary had perceived the preciousness of having him with them. And besides, her anointing would serve as a burial ointment. The ointment that Mary had kept for this occasion would keep until the day of his burial, and, in effect, serve as the ointment used for his burial.[1]

Judas Iscariot is set as a foil against Mary. His impure motives make her pure motives shine. Judas had a habit of "lifting"[2] (pilfering) what was put in the money bag. He was a thief who really had no compassion for the poor, and yet Jesus entrusted the common purse to him (see 13:29). The love of money was very likely Judas' tragic flaw, a flaw that made him susceptible to "sell out" Jesus for thirty pieces of silver.

Having heard of the miracle of Lazarus' resurrection and now discovering that Jesus had returned to be with Lazarus, a large multitude of Jews from the area had come to see both of them. Jesus and Lazarus had become quite an attraction! This aroused the chief priests, "who made plans to kill Lazarus also, for on account of him many Jews were going away and believing in him." The chief priests had already formulated a plan to kill Jesus (11:50–53); now they added Lazarus. His presence, as the one resurrected by the man they wanted to kill, was an embarrassment to them. Many Jews were "going away" (i.e., leaving their allegiance to Judaism and to the Jewish religious leaders) and "were believing in Jesus." This was but the beginning of the great exodus many would take; they left Judaism to follow Jesus.

The next day Jesus made his so-called triumphal entry into Jerusalem. The people were hailing him, crying out, "Hosanna, Blessed is he who comes in the name of the Lord, even the King of Israel!" As they shouted "Hosanna" (from Hebrew, meaning "save now"), they were expecting that the conquering Messiah had come to save them from Roman captivity. To their way of thinking, the one "who comes in the name of the Lord" would be "the *King* of Israel" (see Ps. 118:25–26; Zeph. 3:15). The people were hailing the arrival of their King! Indeed, their King was coming to them—but not the kind of king they expected. Rather, Jesus came to them in the way prophesied by Zechariah:

> Behold your king is coming to you;
> he is just and endowed with salvation,
> Humble and mounted on a donkey,
> Even on a colt, the foal of a
> donkey. (9:9, NASB)

The King, in this coming, would not be a conqueror, but a humble servant. And he would not be exalted to the Davidic throne, but lifted up on Calvary's cross. The Passover Lamb had come to be slaughtered; the grain of wheat had come to be buried. Of course, the people at that time could never have imagined that his entrance into Jerusalem was an entrance into the throes of death. They never would have thought that Jesus was about to enter into glory via death and resurrection. As they shouted Scriptures from Psalm 118:25–26, they probably never thought that the very same psalm (v. 22) ironically foretold that the cornerstone would be rejected by the builders.

It appeared that the whole world had gone after Jesus! Even the Greeks wanted to see him. That should have been the time for Jesus to seize the hour! But the hour had come for the Son of man to be glorified through death and resurrection. The hour had come for him, like a grain of wheat, to be buried in the earth. He would forego the momentary glory for the eternal. The buried grain would eventually bring forth many grains in resurrection[3]—more fruit than could have been gained had he then and there taken the kingship on earth. How many grains have come from that one seed! If Jesus had not gone to Calvary, he would have remained single and alone, like an unplanted grain. But his burial, like a planting, brought germination and multiplication. Jesus, through being lifted up on the cross, would draw all men to himself.[4] His cross, like a charged magnet, would draw millions and millions to him. This has been evidenced by the history of the last two millennia. How many have been drawn to Christ!

The Greek word underlying "draw" is the same word used for drawing in a fishing net. Fishermen throughout the ages have used large dragnets to catch many fish. For example, in Ghana it takes a team of several men on shore at least three hours to draw in the net—after having let it out about three hundred yards into the Atlantic Ocean. On shore, two groups of strong young men, while chanting in syncopation, pull, in unison, the net to shore. The two lines are wrapped around the trunks of the palm trees, fitting into the grooves that have been made there before. Gradually, the two lines are brought together and crossed over. Finally, amidst the screams of gulls and pounding of the surf, a net full of fish is brought to shore. Those fish may have experienced freedom for three hours, but once the net was dropped they were destined to be caught. And so it is for all the believers, who have been captivated by Jesus and drawn to him.

Light in the Darkness (12:37–50)

Following the Lord's proclamations concerning his death and the results it would produce, he gave one final invitation to faith. He asked the people to believe in the light while it was still present. This was their chance to become the sons of light. But most of the Jews, unfortunately, couldn't believe in him. They had believed in a figure called the Messiah—and when Jesus seemed to fit that image, they began to believe in him, but it was difficult to believe him when he continually spoke of his imminent death, and that on a cross. The signs he performed encouraged their faith, but his words about his death shattered the Messianic image. The people had been taught that the Messiah would never die, for he would have an eternal kingdom (see Pss. 89:4; 110:4; Isa. 9:6–7; Dan. 7:14). Consequently, they could not believe that Jesus was the Messiah.

This unbelief was predicted. In the opening of the great chapter on the suffering Savior and sacrificial Lamb, Isaiah declared, "to whom was the arm of the Lord revealed?" (Isa. 53:1). It took revelation from God to see that the suffering, death-bound Jesus was the glorious Lord. But God blinded the Jews and hardened their hearts (see Rom. 11:15) so that they did not see or understand. They did not turn to the Lord and receive his healing. But Isaiah had seen his glory, and because of his vision he predicted the blindness to come (see Isa. 6:1–10). Isaiah had foreseen so much concerning Christ; he was foremost among the prophets to speak of the sufferings of Christ (see chaps. 50, 52, 53) and the glories that followed (see chaps. 6, 9, 11, 40, 60, 61). But he prophesied to a dull people.

Although John tells us that many of the rulers believed in Jesus, they (as well as all the people) did not have Isaiah's vision. If they had, they would not have crucified the Lord of glory (1 Cor. 2:8). Nevertheless, Jesus gave one last appeal to faith, an appeal that summarized the message of his ministry. This would be the Lord's last public proclamation. From then on, all discourse would be between him and his disciples.

In his final message (12:44–50), Jesus reiterated his constant theme that to believe in him was to believe in the Father (see 5:24; 10:38; 14:10–11) and to see him was to see the Father (see 14:8–10). Jesus was God's visible expression on earth; he had come to men to explain and express the Father to them. As such, Christ was the light of the world. Those who believed received the light, but the unbelievers would remain in darkness. Those who believed were those who received the Lord's life-giving words (*rhēmata* in Greek), and those who did not believe were those who rejected his words. Those very words, as a written record (*logos* in Greek), would give judgment against all those who had rejected Christ's speaking.

13

Serving the Believers

John 13:1–30

John 13 opens with a parabolic depiction of the steps in Jesus' journey: from leaving his position as the glorious God, to becoming God's servant as a man, to returning to his glorious state as the God-man. The first step is presented in the description, "he got up from the table, took off his outer robe, and tied a towel around himself." This presents Jesus' willingness to divest himself of deity's privileges and leave his state of glory for the purpose of becoming a servant to men. The next step is described as follows: "Then he poured water into a basin and began to wash the disciples' feet and to wipe them with the towel that was tied around him." This reveals his ministry as God's servant to men. And the final step is as follows: "Then when he had washed their feet, he put on his clothes and reclined again." This completes the symbolic act; it depicts Jesus' return to his former glory after finishing his service to men on earth (see comments on 11:4–5, 6–7). Once willingly divested of coequal glory with the Father in order to be a servant, he now resumes his former position. The entire scene is very close to what Paul verbalized in Philippians 2:5–11. John 13:3–12 provides the portrait, Philippians 2:5–11 the caption.

Jesus, the Servant (13:1–30)

The passage is chronicled as being "before the Passover festival," and the meal that Jesus ate with his disciples was probably the yearly Passover meal, which Jesus and his disciples partook of before the "Lord's Supper" (cf. Matt. 26:17–30; Mark 14:12–26; Luke 22:7–39).[1] This mention of the Passover is symbolic because it speaks of the death of the Passover lamb. Jesus, the true Passover Lamb, was about to be sacrificed; his hour had come.

Jesus was fully aware that his time had come to leave this world and return to his Father, so he devoted his last hours to his disciples, who were those he "loved to the end." The last part of this verse could also be rendered, "he loved them to the utmost." The statement means that Jesus continued his devotion to his disciples until the very end of his life, and "he showed them the full extent of his love" (NIV). Jesus could have been absorbed with his own imminent death; instead, he was concerned for his disciples. They, who had been his companions for over three years, were very dear to him. Before he left them, he wanted to express his love to them, one by one—and this he did by washing each one's feet.

There was a spoiler at this meal, Judas Iscariot, who was about to betray Jesus. Judas had already been in league with the devil and was ready to do his bidding (see 6:70–71 where Jesus calls Judas a "devil"). Thus, the text says, "the devil already had it in his heart [i.e., had resolved] that Judas, son of Simon Iscariot, would betray him." According to the best manuscript evidence, this verse indicates that the devil decided to instigate the actual events of betrayal at that moment. Some scribes changed it to the genitive so as to show that it was Judas' heart, not the devil's, that was affected with the satanic design.[2] In any case, Judas would carry out the devil's plan to kill Jesus.

But Jesus was in control; he had even chosen a man (Judas Iscariot) who was a devil and his betrayer (6:70–71). The betrayal was but a necessary act in the foreordained drama of redemption. Jesus had an absolute knowledge of his origin and destiny. He knew that he had come as God's servant to accomplish redemption, and he knew that he would rise again and return to the Father. His actions that evening illustrated what it meant for him to have come from God and to return to God. The action of rising from supper and setting aside his garment depicted how he, who existed in God's form, equal with God (Phil. 2:6), was willing to divest himself of that reputation. And the action of taking the towel and girding himself with it illustrated how he humbled himself to take the form of a servant. After washing the disciples' feet (a sign of his cleansing ministry), he put his garments on again and returned to his former position. This exhibited his return to glory and to God.

In between the act of rising from his place at the meal and then returning, Jesus washed the disciples' feet and thereby demonstrated his servanthood. (In ancient times, the task of washing guests' feet was a job for a household servant.) All the disciples accepted the washing (perhaps reluctantly but without voicing any protest)—until Jesus came to Peter, who questioned Jesus: "Lord, are you going to wash my feet?" Jesus did not respond to Peter's question; instead, he assured Peter that he would understand the significance of the washing some time in the future. Indeed, after Jesus' crucifixion and resurrection, the disciples understood the significance of what Jesus had said and done. But at the time, Peter refused to let Jesus wash his feet. Jesus told him, "If I do not wash you, you have no part with me." Then Peter wanted a bath! But a bath is not necessary for one who has been bathed, for such a one is completely clean except for his feet.[3] What a bathed person needs is a footwashing.

In speaking to Peter, Jesus used two different Greek words (*niptō* and *louō*) to convey two different kinds of washings. The two washings, one initial and the other continual, are very important to the Christian life. The Greek word *niptō,* appearing in 13:5, 6, 8 and in the last part of 13:10, is used throughout the LXX and New Testament to indicate the washing of the extremities (i.e., the hands and the feet). *Louō* (from which is formed the perfect participle *lelouomenos* in 13:10) specifically means bathing. According to the customs of those times, once a person had bathed his body, he needed only to wash his feet before partaking of a meal. Jesus was going around to all the disciples washing their feet until Peter protested. In his response to Peter, Jesus appropriately used both words in order to advance a precious truth: As he who has been bathed needs only to wash his feet daily, so he who has been bathed by the Lord needs only to wash himself day by day from the filth and defilement that he accumulates by his contact with the world.

All the disciples except Judas, the betrayer, had been cleansed by Jesus. This cleansing probably indicates the washing of regeneration through Jesus' Spirit and word (see John 15:3; Eph. 5:26;

Titus 3:5). John 6:60–71 helps us see that eleven of the disciples had received Jesus' words as spirit and life, but one hadn't—Judas, the devil and betrayer. He was not clean.

Besides the spiritual significance contained in the Lord's word about the two kinds of washing, the act of washing the feet demonstrated the service of love. Jesus, the Teacher and Master, had stooped to a position of humility and service because he loved those he served. Jesus commanded his disciples to serve one another in love and humility, according to the example he set (see 1 Pet. 5:5). And since his action of footwashing ultimately pointed to the forgiveness and cleansing of sins, Jesus' admonishment to act as he did was an encouragement for the disciples to forgive one another and submit to one another. It was their position to be subservient to one another, even as Jesus had been subservient to his Father and was the perfect embodiment of servitude.

But Jesus' statements about serving one another and loving one another did not apply to all of his disciples because, in fact, one of his disciples (Judas) was about to betray him. However, this betrayal was not an unexpected event, for Jesus had known from the beginning that one of the men he chose would betray him (see 6:70–71), and Jesus' betrayal was necessary to fulfill Scripture—specifically, Psalm 41:9, which says "the one eating bread with me has lifted up his heel against me."[4] Psalm 41 is a very fitting portion of Scripture for Jesus to draw prophecy from, because it describes how one of David's companions, perhaps Ahithophel, had turned against him. This was a cause of deep distress for Jesus. The text says, he "was distressed in his spirit." He was deeply affected by the betrayal, even though he knew that the betrayal was foreordained—as was his coming crucifixion.

All the disciples were also greatly agitated by Jesus' pronouncement that one of them would betray him. John, the Gospel writer, called here "the disciple whom Jesus loved" (see also 20:2; 21:7, 20), was nearest to Jesus and therefore in a position to ask Jesus to identify the betrayer. Jesus identified the betrayer as the one to whom he would give the piece of bread dipped in a sauce—of dates, raisins, and/or sour wine (cf. Matt. 26:22–25; Mark 14:19–20; Luke 22:23). Usually, this act singled out the guest of honor. But since Judas was the dishonorable one, the act was ironic. Nonetheless, Judas was not thereby publicly exposed to disgrace. Jesus sent him on his horrid task discreetly after he dipped the morsel and gave it to him. At that moment, Satan entered Judas and the betrayal was set in motion.

The disciples thought Jesus was sending Judas out to purchase something for the feast or to give something to the poor because Judas was in charge of the money (see comments on 12:6). This explanation tells us that the disciples had no idea that Judas was going out to betray their Master. John and Peter knew that the betrayer was Judas, but they must not have realized that Judas was going then and there to betray Jesus. If so, Peter would have tried to stop Judas! But none of the disciples thought Jesus' talk about betrayal indicated an imminent event—just as they did not realize that Jesus would die on the cross the next day. But the stage was quickly being set, as was the mood, which is characterized by the final words of this section: "and it was night." With a touch of artistry, John used the actual time of day to capture the mood of the moment. Judas was in darkness, under the control of the prince of darkness, Satan. The disciples must have sensed an ominous darkness taking over. And Jesus' dark moment was at hand. Nonetheless, he knew that he had come from God and was returning to God. A new day would dawn.

14 Preparing the Way to the Father

John 13:31–14:31

In his last discourse Jesus explains to the disciples that his imminent journey through death, resurrection, and ascension is necessary to prepare the way for the disciples to live in God. This discourse begins at 13:31. Prior to 13:31, Jesus and the disciples shared the Passover meal; Jesus washed their feet, taught them the meaning of the act, and then announced his betrayal. Once Judas went out to betray him, the Lord knew that his crucifixion and resurrection were imminent; he knew he was about to be glorified. Anticipating his glorification, he utters the proleptic proclamation in 13:31: "Now is [lit. was] the Son of Man glorified and God is [lit. was] glorified in him."

This glorification is the keystone of the discourse that follows, which is built upon the fact that Jesus viewed his glorification, via death and resurrection, as accomplished. As a result of this glorification, Jesus in resurrection would acquire a spiritual form that would enable him to indwell his disciples and they to dwell in him. In other words, the essential thing to keep in mind when reading John 14 (and the following chapters) is that most of the discourse is framed in terms of Christ's anticipation of his resurrection and what that resurrection would generate in respect to his spiritual union with the disciples. Indeed, in John 15 the Lord envisions himself and the disciples already organically united as Vine and branches, for he says, in the proleptic present tense, "I *am* the vine, you *are* the branches." This, of course, could not be realized until the Lord in resurrection imparted his life to his believers (see 14:19). On the evening of the resurrection the Lord would come to his disciples and breathe the Spirit into them (20:22), and from then on he would live in them and they in him. The references to his "coming" in chapters 14–16 are not to the second advent per se, but to his coming to them in resurrection. His absence from the disciples would be only for "a little while" (16:16). Then (after three days), they would see him again and rejoice, for on that day, the day of his resurrection, they would know that they were in him and he in them.

Though what I have just cursorily introduced will be detailed when John 14 is explicated, it is necessary that the exegetical construct be established, a construct that is contextually Johannine, not one that is presupposed. We must use the text of John to exegete each passage in John 14 as much as possible, and not some other artificial pretext. But it seems that many commentators superimpose a non-Johannine view to their interpretation of John 14 (especially the first few verses).

The ultimate destiny of the spiritual journey is fully described in Jesus' last discourse. For the Israelites, their ultimate destiny was to enter the good land wherein they would build a house for the glorious God to inhabit. In parallel fashion, John 14 and 15 reveal Jesus' design to prepare a spiritual house wherein God could indwell his believers and have his glory manifest among them.

Jesus' Glorification (13:31–38)

Now that Judas was on his way to betray Jesus into the hands of those who would have him crucified, Jesus looked past the cross to his glorification in resurrection. Anticipating his glorification, Jesus made the proleptic proclamation, "Now is [lit. was] the Son of man glorified, and God is [lit. was] glorified in him." In other words, Jesus viewed his glorification as an accomplished fact. The text goes on to say, "And God will also glorify him in himself, and will glorify him immediately."[1] Speaking of the Son's glorification, Westcott said, "Even as God was glorified in the Son of Man, as man, when he took to himself willingly the death which the traitor was preparing, so also it followed that God would glorify the Son of Man in his own divine Being, by taking up his glorified humanity to fellowship with himself."[2]

Jesus would be going to the Father (14:6, 28) to rejoin him in that sphere of fellowship and glory the Father and Son enjoyed from all eternity (see 17:5, 24 and comments). The disciples would not be able to join him in that fellowship just yet. As Jesus had told the Jewish leaders earlier (see 7:33–34), he now tells his disciples that though they seek him, they will not find him. Not understanding this, Peter wanted to know where Jesus was going. Again, Jesus said, "you are not able to follow me now"—to which he adds, "you will follow me later." Jesus' statement has two meanings: (1) Peter would later follow Jesus in the way of death (see 21:15–19 and comments), and (2) Peter would later follow Jesus into glory.

Peter's response is insightful: "Lord, why can't I follow you now? I will lay down my life for you." Peter must have realized that Jesus' words about his departure indicated that Jesus was about to die, for Peter expressed his willingness to die in Jesus' stead. The statement "I will lay down my life for you" repeats what Jesus said in 10:11, 15, 17 about laying down his life for his sheep. Jesus would really do this; Peter would not. When the time of trial came, Peter would deny Jesus three times (cf. Matt. 26:69–75; Mark 14:66–72; Luke 22:31–34). Jesus clearly predicted this: "before the cock crows, you will have denied me three times" (NRSV). This prediction silenced Peter; in the rest of the discourse, he says nothing. The next time Peter speaks is when he denies knowing Jesus (see 18:17, 25–27).

The time had come in Jesus' journey to return to the Father via death, resurrection, and ascension. In so doing, he was preparing the way for the disciples to have spiritual access (i.e., access through the Spirit) to the Father and for the Triune God to be able to live in the disciples. But the time had not yet come for the disciples to have the same kind of direct access and fellowship with the Father that the Son was about to have. They had their own journeys to take before they would participate in the same; they, too, would have to pass through death and resurrection before they could enjoy eternal, unhindered fellowship.

Jesus, the Way to the Father (14:1–14)

The first portion of John 14 traditionally has been interpreted with the understanding that verse 2 refers to God's house in heaven. Accordingly, most translators have rendered the opening verses of John 14 on the premise that Jesus was speaking about his Father's house in heaven, to which he had to go in order to prepare some rooms and from which he would return one day to take back his believers to be with him in heaven. The day of that return usually has been designated as the second advent (or perhaps the Lord's personal visitation to each believer when he or she departs this world—a favorite homily at funerals).

This exegesis has serious problems. First, "heaven" is not mentioned in John 14. Second, the going away and coming again according to the context of John 14–16 would be but for "a little while" (see 14:19–20; 16:16–23), not two or more millennia! Indeed 14:20 and 16:20–22 make it more than evident that "that day" would be the day of Christ's resurrection, the day in which the disciples, rejoicingly, would realize that they had become united to the resurrected Christ. Third, John 14:4 and 6 indicate that Jesus was talking about the believers coming to the Father through him, the unique way. Surely this access to the Father is not reserved for the second advent or for the time of each saint's departure from this world. Jesus came to provide believers with a way to approach and inhabit the Father here and now (see Eph. 2:18). Fourth, John 14:2–3 reveals that Jesus' intention was to bring the disciples to be with him "where I am," not "where I will be." Where was the Lord then and there? Jesus repeatedly indicated that he was in the Father (10:38; 14:10–11), and he prayed in John 17 that the disciples would also be with him in the Father (vv. 21–24). Of course, the Lord also indicated that he was going to the Father (14:12; 16:28) and that that ascent would take him to heaven. As such, it could be inferred that he was going to heaven, and that was where he wanted to take his disciples. But this misses the mark. The goal of Jesus' mission, according to the Gospel of John, was to express the Father to humankind and to bring the believers to the Father. John 14:6 says it so clearly: "I am the way and the truth and the life; no one comes to the Father except through Me."

The traditional exegesis of John 14:2–3 has serious defects. Some modern commentators have attempted to resolve the problems by suggesting that this little pericope has several layers of meaning. It could indicate (1) the Lord's second advent and the believers' ascent to heaven; (2) the believers' ascent to heaven at the time of death; or (3) the believers' immediate access to God the Father through the Son. Of the three possible meanings, the first is very non-Johannine, although possible. The second is highly unlikely (the Scriptures nowhere speak of the Lord coming again and again for each deceased believer). Only the third, in my opinion, is valid. Nevertheless, most commentators think Jesus was talking about going to a place (heaven) and not to a person (the Father).

There are some commentators, however, who allow for a double interpretation of the text. They consider Jesus' "coming again" as referring to both the resurrection and the parousia—the former foreshadowing the latter. Those who hold this view, therefore, extract a double meaning from Jesus' words in 14:2–3; they say the passage speaks both of the believers being brought into the risen Christ as the many abodes in the Father's house and of the believers being brought by the returned Christ into the Father's house in heaven. Gundry's position represents this view:

> The two meanings illustrate the proleptic theology of John, the tension and correspondence between the already and the not yet. According to the first meaning Jesus speaks of his going to the cross, his preparing by his death spiritual abodes in the Father's household or family, his return to the disciples immediately after his resurrection, and the sending of the Spirit to minister his continuing presence until he comes to receive those who are already in him so that they may be with him eternally. And all of that anticipates the second meaning according to which Jesus speaks of his going to the house of heaven, his preparing there abodes for believers, his return, and his taking believers to be with him in heaven forever since they have already come to be in him by faith. In the last point the two meanings merge.[3]

This interpretation is satisfactory because it allows for a dual significance to the "house" Jesus was going to prepare. However, I would still argue that the notion of a heavenly mansion seems foreign to the context of John. When Jesus said that he was going to prepare a place for the disciples in the Father's house, could he not have been suggesting that he himself was that house? Did not the Father dwell in him, and he in the Father? Then, the way for the disciples to dwell in the Father would be for them to come and abide in the Son. In other words, by coming into the One who was indwelt by the Father, the believers would come simultaneously into the Indweller, the Father. Clearly, this was the Lord's desire and design (see 14:20; 17:21–24). Therefore, when he said he was going to prepare a place for them, does it not mean that he, through the process of death and resurrection, was going to make himself ready to be inhabited by his disciples? If this is not the meaning, what else is?

When Jesus spoke of preparing rooms for the Father's house in heaven he also may have been speaking of preparing resurrection bodies. Paul spoke of this body in terms of it being a heavenly body. He said, "We know that when the earthly tent we live in is destroyed, we have a building from God, a house not made with hands, eternal in the heavens" (2 Cor. 5:1). Jesus himself "prepared" the resurrection bodies by becoming the prototype, the firstfruits of all to follow (1 Cor. 15:23). All Christians will receive a glorified body like Christ's (Phil. 3:21). In this glorious state, Christians will experience perfect union with the risen Christ.

The Gospel of John constantly presents the view that God and man are to mutually indwell each other. As the Father and Son enjoyed co-inherence (mutual indwelling), so the believers were to be brought into the participation of a similar mutual indwelling: the Father in the Son indwelling the believers, and the believers in the Son indwelling the Father. In John 14 the mutual indwelling is inorganic—it is spoken of in terms of abodes; in John 15 it becomes organic—it is spoken of in terms of vine and branches. Either way, John's Gospel focuses on the matter of God and man obtaining an abode in each other.

Let us come back to John 14:2. Isn't the Father's house none other than Jesus? The same expression, "My Father's house," appears in John 2:16, in which it is clear that the temple in Jerusalem was the Father's house; yet in the next few verses (vv. 17–21) Jesus likens *himself* to the temple, a temple that would be destroyed and raised again in three days. Thus, the Son, through the process of crucifixion and resurrection, would become the temple, the Father's house, *prepared* to receive the believers. He, as the temple, as the Father's house, would be the means through which the believers could come to dwell in the Father and the

Father in them. In other words, the Son would become the common abode of the believers and God.

One problem some may find with the interpretation I have proposed is the phrase "many abodes." How could the Lord house many abodes? Answer: the same way in which the Vine incorporates many branches. Note, the Lord does not say, "In my Father's house, there *will be* [future tense] many abodes," but there "*are* [present tense] many abodes." This was spoken proleptically, as also was John 15:2. The believers are viewed as having already inhabited the Son, or as having already been joined to him. Yet this could not be actualized until after the Lord's death and resurrection. It required preparation. Therefore, though the believers are viewed as already being abodes in the Father's house, a place needed to be prepared for them. Once the Lord rose from the dead, God's house would be enlarged from one individual abode (i.e., the Father and the Son indwelling each other) to many abodes (i.e., the Father and the Son indwelling many believers and vice versa). The word "abodes" is used only twice in the entire New Testament, both places in John 14 (vv. 2 and 23). Could the "abodes" be different abodes? According to John 14:23 each believer becomes an abode of the Father and the Son, and since there are many believers, these must be the many abodes in the Father's house. In verse 2, the abodes are spoken of as already existing; in verse 23, we see how these abodes actually come into existence.

I don't think my interpretation is a case of overreading or misguided exegesis. I believe the context of John's Gospel, and especially of chapters 14–17, bears this out. Notice in verse 3 the Lord does not say, "I am coming again and will receive you to *heaven*," but "I am coming again and will receive you to *Myself*." A person, not a place, is the destination. However, the NEB translation of verse 2 indicates that the Lord would be "going there"—to a place, obviously heaven. Furthermore, the translation in NIV failed to relate in verse 3 that the Lord said he would receive the disciples *to himself*. And most translators, under the conception that the Lord was talking about his second advent, rendered a Greek present tense verb (*erxomai*—"I am coming") as an English future, "I will come."

The present tense Greek verb shows the immediacy of the Lord's coming back. His coming to them again would be realized in a short while. (This is confirmed by John 16:16—note the similar use of "again.") When Jesus said, "I am coming again," that "coming again" came on the day of his resurrection. But most translations sound as if that coming is still in the future: "I will come back" (NIV, TEV) or "I will come again" (RSV, NASB, NEB).

Several translations of 14:4 manifest other expansions that are based upon the traditional exegesis explained previously. The translators of NIV, TEV, and NEB added words that indicate that the Lord was going *to a place:* NIV ("the *way to the place*"), TEV ("the way that leads *to the place*"), and NEB ("my way *there*"—a little less conspicuous). But, in context and in accordance with Johannine thought, the Lord was preparing the way through himself to the Father. The destination is not a place but a person. God is the destination, and the Son is the way to him: "I am the way and the truth and the life; no one comes to the Father except through me" (14:6).

In the first six verses of John 14 Jesus has revealed the great truth that he is the unique way to the Father. In verse 7 and following, he will begin to unveil that he is the visible manifestation of the Father. If the disciples were to realize that coming to dwell in the Son was equivalent to coming to dwell in the Father, they would have had to realize that the Son was the Father seen, the manifestation of the Father (see John 1:18; Col. 1:15; Heb. 1:3). If they had come to know the Son, they should have perceived the Father also.

Another manuscript reading yields a translation like the one in TEV: "If you have come to know me, you shall know my Father also."[4] But the entire context of this portion asserts the opposite. It is not that the disciples *will* come to know the Father as they have known the Son, but that they should have already known the Father as manifest in the Son. The Lord was reproving them, not promising them some future knowledge of the Father. If he was making a promise, how could the Lord say in the very next sentence: "And from now on you know him and have seen him" (14:7b)! No, the Lord was not promising but reproving them, due to their lack of discernment—as again, 14:9 asserts: "Jesus said to him, have I been so long with you and you have not come to know me, Philip? He who has seen me has seen the Father."

According to Philip's concept, the Father was another person besides Jesus, a person who could perhaps show up in the room if Jesus called upon him to do so. But the Son and Father are ever inseparable; and it is impossible to show the Father outside of the

Son, for the Son has always been his unique expression. Philip and the disciples should have come to know and recognize that the One in their midst was the very expression of God the Father.

To know the Son is to know the Father and vice versa, because the two exist in one another: "I am in the Father and the Father is in me." This co-inherence is the basis of the oneness between the Father and Son (see 10:30, 38; 17:21–24). The reason the Son could boldly assert that seeing him was equivalent to seeing the Father is that he and the Father are one by virtue of their co-inherence. This vital co-inherence makes it possible for the believers to be in the Father and the Father in the believers, because once the believers enter the Son they come into the Father and the Father comes into them.

The first part of John 14 focuses on God being man's habitation; the second part (beginning with v. 16) centers on man becoming God's habitation. In the first part of the chapter, Jesus revealed his relationship with the Father because the disciples needed to see that their union with the Son meant union with the Father—for the two are one. In the second part Jesus revealed his relationship with the Spirit because his union with the Spirit is the Son's way of indwelling the believers. Jesus himself provides man with the way to access God, and the Spirit gives God a way to access man. Therefore, indwelling the Son equals indwelling the Father, and being indwelt by the Spirit equals being indwelt by the Son.

In 14:16 Jesus said that the Father would give the disciples "another Consoler" (or, "another Comforter"). The expression "another Comforter" *(allon paraklēton)* means "another comforter of the same kind as the first." This, of course, implies that Jesus was the first Paraclete (see 1 John 2:1), and the Spirit would be the same kind of Paraclete. Although it is difficult to reproduce in English the Greek word *paraklētos,* it fundamentally denotes the office of one who comes to the aid of a person in need (lit. one who comes to [our] side when called upon—from *para* [by the side] and *klē-tos* [called]). Properly speaking, this is the office of an Advocate; but this title hardly suits the context of John 14 (cf. 1 John 2:1, where the title "Advocate" is very fitting). Titles like Comforter, Helper, Counselor, or Consoler fit the context of John 14; but neither one by itself seems to be adequate because a Paraclete does more than comfort, help, counsel, and console—he also advocates, exhorts, and teaches.

In verse 17 Jesus identifies the Paraclete; he is the Spirit of truth, or better, the Spirit of reality—inasmuch as he is the Spirit who reveals the reality about God (cf. TEV). The world cannot receive (or accept) this Spirit of reality because the world does not see him or know him. And then Jesus declares, "You know him [lit. it], because he abides with you and shall be in you." This statement indicates that (1) the Spirit embodied in Jesus was then and there abiding *with* the disciples, and (2) the same Spirit of Jesus would, in the future, be *in* the disciples. In other words, the One who was with them would be *in* them. Notice the shift of pronouns from verse 17 to verse 18: "*he* shall be in you . . . I am coming to you." Who is the "he"? The Comforter, the Spirit of reality. Who is the "I"? Jesus, the Son. Who would be coming to them? The Spirit or Jesus? Not either/or; both as one. Notice that further on, in verse 20, the Lord says "I in you." Compare this to verse 17 where Jesus said that the Spirit "shall be in you." Who, then, would be in the disciples?

When we put all these statements together, it should be clear that the Comforter is none other than the Lord as the Spirit. The Comforter who was *with* the disciples was the Spirit abiding in Christ, and the Comforter who would be *in* the disciples was Christ in and as the Spirit. The Spirit of reality coming to the disciples was none other than Christ as the Spirit coming to them; and the Spirit who would be in them would be none other than Christ in them. Morris said, "he [Jesus] comes in the coming of the Spirit."[5]

Not all exegetes will agree with the interpretation presented above, especially those who do their utmost to distinguish the persons of the Trinity. Yet it must be admitted that according to Christian experience, there is no distinguishable difference between the experience of Christ and the experience of the Spirit. The two are one in the same. Paul's practical theology affirms this (see Rom. 8:9–11; 1 Cor. 15:45; 2 Cor. 3:17–18), and so does John's (see 7:37–39; 16:11–13; 20:22). At any rate, the unity between Jesus and the Spirit is essential to the proper interpretation of the Lord's last discourse, and specifically to the verses (16–18) we have been discussing.

After Jesus told the disciples that the Spirit's coming would be his coming to the disciples, he told them that he would not leave them as orphans; he would father them. This coming would be but in "a little while," during which time he would be crucified, buried, and resurrected. The world would never see him again, but they would see him in his resurrection appearances (see 20:20, 26; 21:1, 14). John 16:16–23 makes it more than clear that "the little while" indicates the span of time between Christ's death and resurrection. In resurrection, the living One would become the disciples' life because they would become united to him like branches in the vine: "because I live [timeless and absolute], you also will live." In that day, the day of resurrection, the disciples would come to know (or, realize) that the Son is in the Father, and they are in the Son, and the Son is in them: "I am in my Father and you in Me and I in you."

This is the climax of John 14! Mutual indwelling between God and man is complete! This mutual indwelling is made personal in verses 21 through 23. To anyone who loves the Lord, "he would love him and manifest himself to him" (v. 21). The Greek word underlying "manifest" means "to be brought into light—hence, to appear, to be made visible." The word is used in John 21:1 in connection with the Lord's final resurrection appearance. To the disciples the Lord manifested himself visibly and physically, thereafter, to all his other lovers in his invisible, spiritual presence (see 20:29; 2 Cor. 4:6).

In verse 22 Judas asked Jesus how he was going to reveal himself to the disciples and not to the world. The Greek word behind "to reveal," as a present, active infinitive, denotes a continual act of manifestation, revelation, and disclosure—not just a single event. Indeed, when the Lord relates how he will perform the manifestation, it is evident that the manifestation is not once and for all. To the lover of Jesus, the Son and the Father will come and make a permanent abode with him (v. 23). It does not say, as might be expected by the context of John 14, that the Father and Son make an abode *in* those who love God—for that would imply that the lover is but an instrument, a vessel for God. Though it is true that the believers are God's vessels (see Rom. 9:21), the preposition *para* is used here to indicate a side-by-side, mutual activity, as between two lovers who make a home with each other. The RSV and NIV capture this thought with their rendering, "we will come to him and make our home with him." Earlier in John 14 Jesus revealed how he and the Father were a habitation for the believers; now each believer becomes a dwelling place for the Father and the Son—and the Spirit (see vv. 17–18). The Triune God and the believers secure an abode in and with each other.

15

Planting a New Vine

John 15:1–25

rom God's perspective, the final goal of Israel's journey was to be planted as a vine in the good land of Canaan. This was predicted in the prophetic song of Moses and Israel: "You will bring them and plant them in the mountain of your inheritance, the place, O LORD, which you have made for your dwelling, the sanctuary, O LORD, your hands have established" (Exod. 15:17). The habitation of God in Jerusalem was supposed to be like a fruitful vine, glorifying both God and men. But Israel failed to bear the proper fruit (Isa. 5:1–7; Jer. 2:19–21). Jesus, with his believers incorporated in him, is the true Vine—the true fulfillment of the vine. As the entire race of Israel sprang from the patriarch Israel, the new generation of God's people is here viewed as originating from Christ, organically united to him, as branches emanating from the vine.

Thus, John 15 presents another aspect of the culmination of our spiritual journey; it is a perfect complement to the preceding chapter in that it continues the theme of God and the believers living in each other. Chapter 15 advances the image from an inorganic dwelling to an organic one: "house" and "abodes" become "vine" and "branches." The mutual indwelling expands from a cohabitation to an organic union. And Jesus continues to explain to his disciples how he (as the vine) and they (as the branches) are the true expression of the corporate life that glorifies God the Father.

The Vine and Branches (15:1–16)

In 15:1 Jesus says, "I am the true vine." This does not mean that he, in contrast to the physical vine tree, is the real one. It means that he, in contrast to Israel, who should have been God's vine but failed (Isa. 5:1–7; Jer. 2:19–21), is the *true* Vine—the true fulfillment and actualization of the vine. This, then, becomes the fulfillment of Psalm 80, in which "the Son of man" is said to be the vine planted by God.

The whole race of Israel sprang from the patriarch Israel; the new race of God's people are here viewed as originating from Christ, organically united to him, as branches emanating from the vine— the entire economy being under the care of the Father, the vine-dresser. The union between the vine and the branches is characterized by the expression "in me" and "in you."

But some of the branches need to be cut off. This reminds us of Paul's exposition of Israel's rejection in Romans 11, wherein he speaks of Jews being cut off from the olive tree so that the Gentiles could be grafted in their place. Israel had failed to bear the fruit God required, so there was a need for a removal of the old, dead branches. As such, the branches that are cut off are the Israelites who did not join themselves to Jesus the Vine and therefore died. But the new, grafted-in branches—if they did not bear fruit—could also be cut off. So, the warning applies to Jews and Gentiles alike (see Rom. 11:17–23).

In verses 2 and 3, there are three words whose meanings have troubled translator and exegete alike: *airei, kathairei,* and *katharoi.* The combination of words *airei* and *kathairei*—a definite word play that cannot be matched in English—is fascinating. Most take the first word to designate the action of taking away, though a few would say it means "lift up."[1] Both meanings are present in the New Testament, but can both be true in this verse? Vine-dressers are known to lift up branches from the ground to enhance fruit-bearing, and to clean a dirty vine for the same reason. Perhaps the combination of *airei* and *kathairei* describes this process. However, most commentators understand *airei* to describe cutting off (see 15:6) and *kathairei* to describe pruning.[2] It seems Jesus has moved to a different level of abstraction. Purging, like pruning, is a spiritual cleansing, a taking away of the filth. Verse 3 indicates that the disciples were already clean *(katharoi)* on account of the Lord's word; this purging serves as a pruning and pruning will cause fruit-bearing.

Verse 4 contains the theme of this pericope: "Abide (or, remain) in me, and I in you." Since each branch (believer) has been positioned in the vine, he or she is charged to *remain* in union with Christ, not to *attain* the union. The Greek for "abide" is an imperative *(meinate)*. Here it is constative; it encompasses the entire act of abiding and views it as a single event.[3] Then, in the following sentences, the Lord constantly uses present tense verbs to describe the continual activity involved in maintaining an organic union with Christ.

Each branch that continues to remain in the vine will keep on bearing fruit (v. 5). Some commentators say the fruit is new converts (cf. v. 6), and others, "the fruit of the Spirit" (Gal. 5:22). The devotional writer, Andrew Murray said, "the essential idea of fruit is that it is the silent natural restful produce of our inner life."[4] The fruit is the practical expression of the indwelling divine life. This expression in our lives should attract people to Christ and thus make them new members of God's vine.

Each branch that does not continue to abide in the vine is expelled from the vine. This is a harsh reality, which may or may not imply eternal destruction. Seen within its context, the verse is probably more experiential than doctrinal. The verse deals with the vital necessity of abiding in the vine and the consequences of not doing so. When Israel had failed to be a profitable fruit-bearing vine—not yielding the good fruit of righteousness—God said he would destroy that vine (see Ps. 80:8–16; Isa. 5:5–7; Ezek. 15:2–7; 19:10–14), yet such destruction did not mean eternal perdition for Israel.

On the positive side, Jesus assures fruitfulness to each branch abiding in the vine. However, abiding in the vine could be so subjective and mystical that each believer could determine for himself or herself what it entails. So Jesus equated abiding in the vine with abiding in his word and keeping his commands.[5] Every believer who abides in the Lord's word and keeps his commands will be fruitful (15:7–10). Christians were chosen for this and appointed for this. It is God's design and economy that each believer should live in union with his Son and be fruitful (i.e., express the effect of that union in daily life). This glorifies the Father.

Love among the Believers in a World of Hatred (15:17–25)

Having spoken of the relationship between the vine and each of the branches, Jesus then turned his attention to the relationship between the branches (i.e., the disciples). He commanded them to "love one another." The disciples are to love one another because they will take Jesus' message to a world that despises them. The external hatred should intensify, not diminish, the internal love of the Christian community. The world was on the verge of totally rejecting its God and Savior, Jesus Christ, by assenting to his crucifixion. The same world would surely hate those who proclaim their allegiance to this crucified Lord.

Jesus told them, "If they persecute me, they will also persecute you; if they kept my word, they will also keep yours" (15:20). This proclamation points to the practical unity of the vine with the branches. The life of the believers is intrinsically joined with Christ's; his experience will be theirs—both negatively (through persecution) and positively (through acceptance).

The hatred the Jews had for Jesus would be extended to the apostles because they were Jesus' spiritual extension. The Jewish leaders had rejected the Word, the very revelation of God the Father to men; they had no way to cover up their sin. Their rejection of Jesus caused their sin to be fully exposed. By hating the Son they were actually hating the Father who sent him. The Scripture predicted this rejection and hatred. Psalm 69:4 said, "they hated me without cause." Applying this to his own situation, Jesus indicated that the Jewish leaders hated him for no good reason; their hatred came from jealousy and envy (see Matt. 27:18). In Psalm 35, anticipating Jesus, David expressed the same sentiment; his enemies (spurred on by envious Saul) hated him for no good reason.

16 Sending the Spirit of Reality

John 15:26–16:33

n his last discourse Jesus reveals that his departure will bring the coming of the Spirit (as the invisible presence of Jesus) to encourage the disciples as they live in a hostile world. Even the name Jesus ascribes to the Spirit—the *paraklētos*—describes an advocate and a defender, for he is the one who stands by the believers and defends them against a hostile world. But the Spirit of reality does more than just defend; he is the revealer of divine truths and the conveyer of Jesus' invisible presence. The Spirit brings the Son to the believers, and the Son brings the Father. Thus, the Spirit provides the believers access into the Triune God and the Triune God access to the believers.

Jesus and the Spirit (15:26–16:15 [with 14:26][1])

In 14:26 it was asserted that the Father would send the Paraclete, the Spirit of reality, in the name of his Son, the Lord Jesus Christ. Just as the Son had come in the Father's name (i.e., the Son, as the very embodiment of the Father, came to express the Father), so the Spirit would come in the Son's name, as the embodiment of the Son, to make the Son real in the believers' experience. Perhaps this is why the Spirit in New Testament writings has taken on the name "Lord" ("the Spirit of the Lord," 2 Cor. 3:17–18), "Jesus" ("the Spirit of Jesus," Acts 16:7), "Christ" ("the Spirit of Jesus Christ," Phil. 1:19).

In 15:26 it is stated that the Son would send the Paraclete, the Spirit of reality, from the Father. Who sent the Spirit? The Father

(14:26) or the Son (15:26)? There is actually no contradiction, for the Lord says that he would send the Spirit *from the Father.* In fact, the Lord emphasizes that the Spirit "proceeds out from the Father." Both 14:26 and 15:26 designate the Father as the source from which the Spirit would be sent; 15:26 adds an extra detail: the Son would also send the Spirit. Thus, the Father and Son together would send the Spirit.

In 16:8–11 Jesus declares that the Spirit will convict the world (prove humankind guilty) concerning sin, righteousness, and judgment. He will convict the world (1) of its sin because they do not believe in Jesus (i.e., the world's unbelief is their sin); (2) concerning righteousness because Jesus went to the Father and they would see him no more (i.e., it will now be the Spirit's function to show people that righteousness is in Christ); (3) concerning judgment because the ruler of this world has been judged (i.e., the Spirit will show to humankind that Christ judged Satan).[2] Operating according to what Christ has accomplished, the Spirit convicts people concerning their sin of unbelief in Christ, concerning the righteousness that is found in Christ alone, and concerning the judgment over Satan accomplished by Christ on the cross.

Having indicated what the Spirit would be doing *in the world* (16:7–11), Jesus then related (vv. 13–15) to the disciples what the Spirit would be doing *in the believers.*[3] Verses 13–15 display a sublime picture of the inner workings of the three members of the Godhead, and special detail is given to describe the Spirit's function of conveying the Father and the Son to the believers and of leading the believers into the Son and the Father. Here the Spirit is seen in full submission to and in harmony with the Son and the Father. He does not act or speak from himself; nothing originates from him, for all comes from the Son and all is done to glorify the Son. Just as the Son did not do anything from himself, but only that which he heard and received from the Father (see 5:19, 30; 8:28, 38; 14:10, 24), so the Spirit never acts independently from the Son. The Spirit appropriates the aggregate totality of Christ's person and reveals it, item by item, to the believers. Yet in revealing Christ (and all that he is) the Spirit is actually revealing the Father, because all that Christ has is the Father's. Thus, the Spirit reveals the Son, who, in turn, expresses the Father.

The prominent role of the Spirit of reality is to lead or guide the believers *into* (Greek *eis*) all the reality of Christ (16:13). According to Johannine usage, which seems to follow the classical distinction between *eis* and *en, eis* is used dynamically—indicating penetration into an object, person, or sphere. When the Spirit leads the believers *into* all the truth, he penetrates that sphere for them and guides them into a definite destiny, Christ (who is reality).

In addition to revealing Christ and guiding the believers into the experience of Christ, the Spirit's function is to continue the spoken ministry of Jesus. According to John 14:26, the Spirit would come to carry on Jesus' speaking both by way of teaching and by way of reminding the disciples of what Jesus had said during his ministry. (This reminding enabled the Gospel writers to recall and record the very words of Jesus.) The Spirit would also affirm Jesus' ministry by bearing witness to him (15:26). The Lord had many things he wanted to tell the disciples before he departed from them, but they were not able to bear them. When the Spirit would come, he would speak to the disciples whatever he heard from Jesus (16:12–13).

The Spirit's function throughout the church age has been to continue Jesus' spoken ministry. The Lord via the Spirit still speaks to the churches. In Revelation 2 and 3 *the Lord Jesus* addressed each of the seven local churches, and yet it is said that the churches should hear what *the Spirit* says to the churches (see Rev. 2:1, 7, 8, 11, 12, 17, 18, 29; 3:1, 6, 7, 13, 14, 22). Thus, the Lord who speaks to the churches is the Spirit who speaks to the churches and vice versa, for the Spirit is the speaking Christ.

Jesus Going and Coming (16:16–33)

Since his departure was imminent, Jesus had much he wanted to convey to his beloved disciples, who (by now) must have realized he was earnest about leaving. Yet he knew something they didn't: he would be returning to them very soon. But they were so overwhelmed by their grief over his imminent departure that Jesus had to assure them that the interim between his going and returning would be only for a little while.

The saying "a little while and you will no longer see me, and again a little while and you will see me" (16:16) was troublesome to the disciples. However, they should have realized from Jesus' discourse in chapter 14 that he was speaking of his going to the Father but soon returning to them. The interim between his going and coming would be but for "a little while." Indeed, this "little while" would last only three days, during which time he would go to the cross, arise, ascend to the Father (20:17), and return to the disciples on the evening of the resurrection (20:19–23). In this interim, the Lord would go to the Father and so prepare a place for the believers in him (14:2–3). When he said, "I am coming again" (v. 3) he was not referring to his second coming (as so many surmise) but to his return on the evening of the resurrection. At that time he would receive the disciples to himself so that they could be with him where he was—in the Father (v. 3).

Jesus had already spoken to the disciples about this "little while" in 14:19–20. There he indicated that the disciples would not see him for a little while but then they would see him—and on that day (i.e., the day of resurrection) they would come to realize that he was in the Father, and they in him, and he in them.

Following his explanation of the interim between his going and coming, Jesus used an allegory (see 16:29) to depict how quickly the disciples' grief would turn to joy and to convey a spiritual truth about his death and resurrection: "You will be grieved, but your grief will be turned to joy. When the woman gives birth she is grieved that her hour has come, but when the child is born, she no longer remembers the affliction for joy that a man was born into the world" (16:20–21).

There is more to this allegory than depicting grief turned to joy. The woman's hour of travail corresponds to the "hour" the Lord constantly referred to throughout his ministry, which would be the hour of his glorification via crucifixion and resurrection (see John 2:4; 7:30; 8:20; 12:23–24, 27; 13:1). The "man born into the world" represents Christ who was begotten from the dead (see Acts 13:33–34; Col. 1:18). The travailing woman, according to the context, depicts the grieving disciples who, in a greater sense, represent God's people who had the expectation of being delivered from their sorrows and travails by virtue of Christ's victory over death (see Isa. 26:16–19; and cf. Rev. 12:1–5). He is the *man* born into the world; as such, he is the hope of all humankind. Hermann Olshausen said, "The proper import of the figure seems to be, that the death of Jesus Christ was as it were an anguish of birth belonging to all humanity . . . in which the perfect Man was born into the world; and in this very birth of the new man lies the spring of eternal joy, never to be lost for all, inasmuch as through him and his power the renovation of the whole is rendered possible."[4]

After presenting this allegory, Jesus told the disciples very clearly: "I came forth from the Father and have come into the world; again, I leave the world and go to the Father" (16:28). This was plain speaking! The light finally dawned on them; they believed that Jesus came from God (16:30). But their revelation was not quite up-to-date. What they really needed to see was that Jesus was about to go to the one he came from and then (very soon) return to them. Without this realization, they would not be able to stand with Jesus in his hour of trial. When the Shepherd would be struck, the sheep would scatter.

17

Praying for Oneness

John 17:1–26

A s a conclusion to his last discourse, Jesus makes petition for himself, his disciples, and all who would become believers— that they would be a unified, corporate testimony to all people that God had sent his Son into the world. In this prayer we discover that Jesus wants the believers to share with him in his enjoyment of the Father. The ultimate experience of our spiritual journey is to enter into the same communion the Son had with his Father before the world was.

Long before creation, even from eternity, the Father and the Son enjoyed fellowship with each other. We know this because the Bible tells us so, although not in any great detail. For the most part, the Scriptures are silent about the premundane scene. And yet there are a few verses that lift the veil slightly and give us a glimpse into that sublime, divine relationship that always existed between the Father and the Son.

Of all the books in the Bible, the Gospel of John has the most to say about the relationship between the Father and the Son. It is from John's inspired pen that we read from the outset, "In the beginning was the Word, and the Word was with God, and the Word was God." This is a rather flat rendering. The Greek conveys something more picturesque: "In the beginning was the Word and the Word was face to face with God, and the Word was himself God." Imagine—the Word, who was the preincarnate Son of God, was face to face with God. The Father and Son enjoyed intimate fellowship from eternity. How they must have delighted in each other.

After the Son of God became a man and began his ministry on earth, he would refer to the relationship he enjoyed with the Father before the foundation of the world. Jesus spoke of what he had seen and heard together with the Father before coming to earth (see John 3:11; 8:38). Jesus longed to return to that glorious sphere. In this final prayer before going to the cross (John 17), he asked the Father to glorify him with the glory which he had with the Father before the world was (v. 5). Jesus wanted to recapture his primordial equality with the Father—something he had willingly relinquished for the sake of his Father's plan (see Phil. 2:6–7). As he prayed to the Father, a wonderful utterance escaped from his lips: "Father, you loved me before the foundation of the world" (17:24). God's Son, the unique Son, was the single object of the Father's love.

I believe it was this love for his Son that first inspired God the Father to want to have many more sons—like his first Son. His one Son brought him so much satisfaction that he yearned to have many more. This became the impetus for the creation of the universe and, most specifically, man. Proverbs 8:30–31 indicates that God was delighted with the sons of men. This is again expressed in the New Testament, especially in the Book of Ephesians. The opening verses of Ephesians resound with this note: the heart's desire of God was to obtain many sons in and through his Son. The many sons, in union with the unique Son, would bring great glory and satisfaction to the Father.

The impetus of God's eternal purpose came from a heart's desire,[1] and that heart's desire was to have many sons made like his only Son (see Rom. 8:26–28). In love, he predestined many people to participate in this "sonship"[2]—not by their own merits but by virtue of being in the Son (Eph. 1:4–5). Notice how often in Ephesians 1 Paul speaks of the believers' position "in him." Outside of him (the Son), no one could be a son of God and no one could be pleasing to the Father. The many sons[3] owe all their divine privileges to the Beloved, as ones graced in him (Eph. 1:6). If it were not for God's satisfaction in his beloved Son, there would not have been the inspiration for the creation of man in the first place. We exist because God wanted to obtain many more sons, each bearing the image of God's unique Son. We are well-pleasing to God and bring him satisfaction by being united to the One who has always satisfied him. Apart from the Son, we have no access, no right to sonship. He is our unique way to the Father.

In this final prayer Jesus declares that he will share his glory with the believers; this is the glory of sonship (see John 1:14). By virtue of their union with the Son, the believers can enjoy oneness with one another. Thank God that it was his good pleasure to include us in his Son, to impart to us—the believers—the divine, eternal life, and to extend to us an opportunity to participate in the fellowship that he and his Son enjoyed from eternity.

Jesus' Prayer (17:1–26)

John 17 contains Jesus' sublime, high priestly prayer. This petition, which consummates his discourse begun in 13:31, expresses the deepest desires of God's heart for his chosen ones. The Lord did not pray for the world but for his own. He prayed for that group of men given to him as a gift from the Father, and he prayed for all who would believe on him through *their* word. He requested that all the believers would share with him in his glory and in his relationship with the Father. From eternity, the Father loved the Son and the Son enjoyed coequal glory with the Father. The two were (and are) essentially and co-inherently one. The believers, he asked, should be brought into oneness by virtue of being in the Triune God and the Triune God being in them. Oneness among the believers was to issue from each believer's oneness with God. What a lofty petition!

Jesus began his petition by asking the Father to glorify him so that he might glorify the Father (v. 1). As was stated earlier, Jesus' glorification is the central theme of Jesus' discourse in 13:31–16:33. If the Father would glorify the Son in resurrection, the Son could in turn impart life to the believers (17:2) and so glorify the Father. Of course, Jesus viewed his glorification as certain as history (see 13:31–32); nevertheless, he prayed for that which he believed would most certainly take place.

Jesus made his requests to the Father, knowing that the Father had given him authority over all people and that he could give eternal life to all whom (lit. all which) the Father had given him. As was discussed earlier in connection with John 6:37–39, Jesus used the neuter singular "all which" (Greek *pan ho*) when referring to the one corporate gift of all believers given to him by the Father. But in the same breath he acknowledged the plurality and individuality of the members of that group by using a personal pronoun ("give *them each* eternal life"). (See 17:24 for the same pattern; and see 6:37–40; 10:29–30 for a shift from the one corporate entity to each individual member.) Each and every member of that corporate "gift" would be given the gift of eternal life.

In 17:3 Jesus defined eternal life. To experientially, progressively know God and his Son, Jesus Christ, is eternal life. In other words, eternal life is the ongoing knowledge of the Father and the Son. The Greek verb *ginōskōsin* signifies the continual action of "getting to know." In colloquial English we could render this verse: "And this is eternal life: that they may get to know you, the only true God, and Jesus Christ, whom you have sent."

In verse 4 Jesus affirmed that he had glorified the Father on earth by accomplishing the works he was given to do. Then, in verse 5, he asked that the Father would glorify him with the glory he had with the Father before the world was. In saying this, Jesus lifted the veil to give us a glimpse of his eternal, premundane relationship with the Father. According to a literal interpretation of the Greek, Jesus was asking to be glorified alongside the Father (i.e., in the Father's presence) by means of (or, with) the glory he had with the Father before the world was. In other words, Jesus was praying to enter into that pristine state of coequal glory with the Father, a position he possessed from the beginning as the unique Son of God. He prayed that the same glory would be the means by which he (now as a man) would be brought into that coequal glory with the Father. This is the climax of Jesus' journey: to return to God not just as God, but also as man.

After praying for his own glorification, Jesus turned the direction of his petition to the disciples. Since he would be leaving the world to rejoin the Father and since the disciples would be staying in the world, they needed to be preserved from the evils in the world. Jesus asked that the Father would keep them in the name that the Father had given him[4] so that they would be one, even as the Son and Father were one (vv. 11–12). In short, Jesus requested that the disciples would be sanctified from the world and from the evil one by means of his name (i.e., his person—vv. 11–12), the word (vv. 14–17), and the truth (v. 17). These are the sanctifying elements, the elements that preserve Christians who must live in the midst of an evil world.

After praying for his disciples, Jesus prayed for all those who would believe in him through their word (v. 20). Since the apostles' word became the New Testament Scriptures (for the most part) and the very foundation of the faith (see Eph. 2:20), everyone who has become a believer has done so through the apostles' words. Therefore, Jesus was praying for all the believers that would ever be. This includes you and me and every genuine believer. (How good it is to know that Jesus prayed for me!) First, Jesus prayed for the apostles to be one (17:11) and then he prayed for all the believers, including the apostles, to be one. This is included in the petition, "that they all may be one" (v. 21).

Let us look closely at the three things Jesus requested in verses 21–23. Each request begins with the word "that" (Greek *hina*): (1) "that they all may be one, even as You, Father are in me and I in you"; (2) "that also they may be in us"; (3) "that the world may continually believe that you sent me." All the requests are subsequential: #2 depends upon #1, and #3 depends on both. In the first request, the Lord asked that *all* the believers may be one. This universal and all-encompassing petition includes all the believers throughout time. Then the first request is qualified by an astounding fact: the oneness among the believers is to be *as* the mutual indwelling of the Father and the Son. In other words, as the Father and Son's oneness is that of mutual indwelling (John 10:30, 38; 14:9–11), so the believers are to have a oneness *as* theirs (see 17:11–22). Since the believers cannot indwell each other, their oneness is not exactly the same as the Father and Son's, but in the *same principle* as their oneness—the principle of mutual indwelling. The oneness of the believers would be realized by virtue of the mutual indwelling between each believer and the Triune God— much like each and every branch in the vine is one with all the other branches by virtue of their common participation of abiding in the vine.

In verses 22–23 Jesus defined the oneness in terms of the mutual indwelling: "that they may be one, even as we are one: I in them and you in me, that they be completed in their oneness." In verse

21 Jesus asked that the believers be *in* the Father and Son; in verses 22–23 he asked that the Father in the Son be in the believers. Now the mutual indwelling is complete and perfect. The reality and demonstration of this oneness will convince the world that the Father did indeed send the Son.

In verse 24, Jesus again spoke of "that which" the Father had given him. The term "that which" (Greek *ho*) designates all the believers as the one collective entity given as a gift to him from the Father (see John 6:37, 39; 10:29; 17:2).[5] This is the same corporate group referred to in 17:2; it includes all the ones who have received and will receive the gift of eternal life. This corporate whole, then, is the universal church, the one body of Christ. The Lord requests that each one of that corporate whole may be with him where he is—in glory with the Father. There, in the Father, with the Son, they could view the glory that the Son received from the Father, because he loved him before the foundation of the world.

What a revealing statement: the Father loved the Son before the foundation of the world! Again, Jesus lifted the veil to give us a glimpse of his eternal, preincarnate relationship with the Father. And what is more astounding is that Jesus asked the Father to love the believers with the same love he had for his Son. Jesus asked that the Father's love would be in us and that he himself (Jesus) would be in us. Because of the Father's love, we are indwelt by the Son. "I in them"—what a conclusion to this sublime prayer! It expresses the kernel of God's desire, which is to have his Son (the "I") in a corporate people (the "them"): "I in them."

18 Facing Trial

John 18:1–19:16a

nlike the Synoptic Gospels, the Fourth Gospel provides no account of Jesus' temptation in the wilderness or his agony in the Garden of Gethsemane. This does not mean, however, that John's account has no record of Jesus passing through trial. John 12:27 reveals Jesus' agony over his imminent crucifixion, and John 13:21 recounts his distress concerning his betrayal by Judas Iscariot. All the Gospel writers agree on one point: any and all of Jesus' trials reveal his perfection. No matter what stress Jesus encountered, he did not collapse. Rather, he endured with majestic resiliency. As the writer of Hebrew says, "God made the pioneer of our salvation perfect through suffering" (2:10).

Thus, God allowed Jesus to face trial before the Jewish high priest and the Roman procurator because these trials would show that Jesus was found guiltless by both the Jewish and Roman authorities. The high priest could not accuse Jesus of having done anything wrong (see 18:23–24), and Pilate openly declared, "I find no fault with him" (19:4). Nevertheless, Jesus, without any sin charged against him, was crucified for the sins of the world. How ironic and symbolic that Jesus was arrested, tried, and crucified while the Passover lambs were being slain in Jerusalem for the Passover meal. A lamb had to be without blemish before it could qualify as a Passover sacrifice. Jesus, the perfect Lamb, was found faultless and then was slain for us.

Jesus' Arrest (18:1–11)

After the last discourse, Jesus went with his disciples to the Garden of Gethsemane, located outside the eastern wall of the city, at the foot of the Mount of Olives. In order to get to the Garden of Gethsemane, they had to cross "the ravine of the Kidron." This ravine, filled with water-torrents during the winter, was now dry. It was either by coincidence or design that David also crossed the Kidron as he departed Jerusalem in his flight from Absalom (see 2 Sam. 15:23). Both had been betrayed: David by Ahithophel and Jesus by Judas. But both would return to Jerusalem: David as a revived king and Jesus as the risen Lord.

Judas, the betrayer, was about to carry out his treachery to the end. Knowing that Jesus would go to Gethsemane with his disciples (for Jesus had often met there with his disciples—see Luke 21:37), Judas guided a platoon of Roman soldiers and some officials from the chief priests and Pharisees to the garden. The Jewish leaders must have asked the Romans for their help in arresting Jesus because their ultimate intention was to procure their assistance in executing Jesus.

When the time had come for Jesus to hand himself over to his executioners, he boldly identified himself. When they asked him if he was Jesus the Nazarene, he responded, "I am he." Some commentators consider this response to be a declaration of deity (as in 8:58). It can't be denied that these words had a profound effect on Jesus' arrestors; they all fell to the ground when they heard these words. In any event, this display of power shows that Jesus could have exercised his power to thwart his arrest, but chose not to.

Jesus' Trials (18:12–19:16a)

The Jews and the Roman cohort, led by a commander, arrested Jesus, bound him, and brought him to Annas. Annas had been deposed as the Jewish high priest by the Romans in A.D. 15, but he still exerted great influence over the ruling high priest, his son-in-law, Caiaphas. And he still retained the title "high priest" as an emeritus title. Very likely, Annas had asked to interrogate Jesus, and was given the first rights to do so (see 18:19–23). Caiaphas is further identified for John's readers as the one who had previously advised the Jews that it was expedient for one man to die on behalf of the people (see 11:49–50).

While Annas was interrogating Jesus, Peter was defending himself with false denials (18:15–18, 25–27), just as Jesus had predicted (13:37–38; cf. Matt. 26:33–35; Mark 14:29–31). Was this the behavior of a coward or did Peter deny knowing Jesus so that he could stay near Jesus and perhaps rescue him from his enemies? Either way, Peter realized he had utterly failed. This was a major crisis in Peter's life—one that completely devastated him. Only an appearance from the risen Lord could help him recover (see Chapter 20).

In the meanwhile, Annas continued to interrogate Jesus but to no avail. He really couldn't find anything to blame Jesus for, nor did Annas have an answer to Jesus' challenge: "If I spoke inaccurately, point out what is wrong" (18:23). So Jesus was sent on to Caiaphas and then on to Pilate.[1] The Jews bringing Jesus to Pilate "did not enter the Praetorium so that they wouldn't be defiled, but would be able to eat the Passover" (18:28). Ironically, Jesus' accusers were concerned about defiling themselves in the house of a Gentile at the very moment they were rejecting God's true Passover Lamb (Isa. 53:4–7; 1 Pet. 1:18–20).

From the onset it was clear to Pilate that the Jewish leaders really didn't have a case against Jesus. He wanted to dismiss the matter as one pertaining to religious law, but they gained Pilate's attention by insinuating that they had already found Jesus worthy of death by their own law but were not permitted to put him to death. Under Roman rule, the Jews were not allowed to carry out any execution without their sanction. Thus, the Jews needed the Romans to execute Jesus for them. Jesus knew this all along, for he had predicted that he would die by the cross—the Roman method of executing non-Romans. The Jewish leaders had attempted to stone Jesus for blasphemy and failed (see 8:59; 10:31); now they wanted the Romans to kill Jesus for them by crucifying him. If Pilate assented, this would serve them well because it would give the appearance to the Jewish populace (who was enamored with Jesus at the moment) that the Roman leaders (not the Jewish leaders) were responsible for his death.

But Pilate would not easily give his approval; he wanted to question Jesus for himself. When Pilate asked Jesus if he were the king of the Jews, Jesus said, "My kingdom is not of this world. If my kingdom were of this world, my servants would have fought to prevent me from being handed over to the Jewish leaders. But my kingdom is not of this world" (18:36). Pilate responded, "So then you are a king." Yes, but not the kind Herod was or Pilate wished he was. Jesus replied, "You said it—I am a king.[2] For this I was born and came into this world—to testify to the truth. Everyone who is of the truth hears my voice" (v. 37).

Pilate, unable to comprehend the meaning of "truth," was still capable of seeing that Jesus was truly not guilty of any crime. Pilate's intention was to teach Jesus a lesson by scourging him and then to release him (see John 19:1; Luke 23:16, 22). He thought the scourging would appease the Jews. But the Jewish leaders were adamant. They demanded Jesus' death. But Pilate countered: "I bring him out to you that you may know that I find he is not guilty of any crime" (19:6). After Jesus' beating and the display of mockery, Pilate, for a second time (see 18:38), declared Jesus "not guilty"—that is, not guilty of a crime warranting death. Pilate even taunted the Jewish leaders by saying, "You take him and crucify him, for I find him not guilty of any crime" (19:6). Thus, Pilate dared the Jewish leaders to usurp the exclusive Roman authority of capital punishment by crucifying their "King" themselves.

The Jewish leaders were too shrewd to fall into this trap. Their retort was, "We have a law, and by our law he ought to die, because he made himself the Son of God" (v. 7). The irony here is that the Jews appealed to Pilate to punish Jesus with Roman crucifixion for violating a strictly Jewish law! But when Pilate heard this, he was even more afraid. Since Romans were inclined to believe in human deities, Pilate took this statement seriously—and perhaps he intuitively sensed that the man in his presence was more than just a human being. Driven by this sense, Pilate wanted to question Jesus even further. But Jesus made no reply. Frustrated, Pilate gave Jesus an ultimatum: "Don't you know that I have the authority to release you and the authority to crucify you?" To which Jesus replied, "You have no authority at all unless it has been given to you from above" (v. 11).

In this one statement, Jesus revealed that a greater authority than Caesar's (who vested Pilate with the power of capital punishment) was at work in all of this. God was making all things work for the purpose of bringing Jesus to the cross. In this regard, Pilate was not completely guilty. The one who delivered Jesus over to Pilate was guilty of a greater sin. This person was Caiaphas, the high priest who had just handed Jesus over to the Romans. For a Jewish high priest to deliver the Jews' King and Messiah over to the Romans for execution was a more heinous sin than for the Roman governor to sentence him to death.

By this time Pilate was apparently convinced that Jesus was some kind of extra-special, supernatural person, so he tried still another time to let him go. But the Jews were not about to let Jesus escape at this point in the trial, so in a final desperate ploy they appealed to Pilate's friendship with Caesar: "If you release this man, you are not a friend of Caesar. Anyone who claims to be a king opposes Caesar." Since most Jews despised the Roman ruler, this was utter hypocrisy; but their hatred for Jesus led them to this lie. At any rate, their ploy worked—for Pilate was probably afraid that he would be reported to Caesar as having released a man who had been charged with sedition. Ironically and symbolically, Pilate sentenced Jesus to death at the same time the Passover lambs were being slaughtered, which was on the day of the preparation for the Passover (i.e., on Friday) some time before noon. Again, this points to Jesus as the Passover Lamb.

But it was not Pilate who was responsible for Jesus' death. Caiaphas and the Jewish leaders were. That is why the text says, "so Pilate handed him over to them to be crucified." According to the grammatical structure of the Greek text, the pronoun "them" refers to the "chief priests" in 19:15; but it was the Roman soldiers who actually carried out the crucifixion. The ambiguity was intentional; John wanted his readers to realize that it was the Jewish leaders who were ultimately responsible for Jesus' death, even though the Romans performed the execution.[3]

All in all, Jesus' trials were blatant scams. He was sentenced to be crucified without any charges against him. This would have never happened if God had not allowed it to happen. Jesus was destined to die on the cross for our sins.

19

Dying on the Cross

John 19:16b–37

oes John veil Jesus' suffering behind a veneer of deity? In a
sense, he does. We see no agony in the garden, and we hear
no beseeching cries from the cross. We see a man who is
always aware that he has an appointed hour to die. This
deeply troubles him (see 12:27–28; 13:21), and yet his death
sentence liberates him. Knowing he has no future life on earth, he
abandons himself to his Father and to doing his Father's will. At
the same time, he greatly anticipates the coming hour of
glorification. The cross would release him from human bondage.

Jesus submitted to his betrayal and crucifixion without any hes-
itation. Having a complete foreknowledge of what was to come and
being fully cognizant that all things would happen as they had been
predetermined, Jesus unswervingly walked into his own death.
Unlike the presentation in the other Gospels, there is no question
about whether or not he would drink the cup the Father had given
him (18:11). He would do as the Father had commanded. He would
go, like a lamb, to his death.

Jesus' Crucifixion (19:16b–37)

All the things that happened in connection with Jesus' betrayal
and crucifixion transpired according to the prearranged, divine
plan. The hour was predetermined; it could not happen before or
after the Passover. The betrayer, Judas Iscariot, was picked by

Jesus. He knew from the beginning that Judas was a devil and would be his betrayer (see 6:64, 70). The method of death—crucifixion—was prearranged, so Jesus knew that he would be lifted up on the cross (see 12:32–33). Thus, it was clear that his executors would be the Romans (for they were the unique administrators of this kind of capital punishment) and not the Jews, who executed by stoning (18:32). The Jews attempted to stone Jesus many times, but they never succeeded because it was not in accord with the divine plan.

Many of the events that occurred during his arrest and crucifixion were destined to happen because they had been prophesied. Only Jesus was arrested, not one of his disciples, in fulfillment of the Scripture, "Of those whom you have given me I lost not one" (18:9, from John 6:39). When Jesus was on the cross, the soldiers cast lots for his tunic without realizing that they were carrying out a part of predictive prophecy (19:24, from Ps. 22:18). But Jesus knew that what was transpiring was in accord with God's predetermined will. Near the end of his crucifixion Jesus, "knowing that all things had now been accomplished," said, "I thirst." This fulfilled the Scriptures (19:28, from Ps. 69:21). After Jesus died, the soldiers refrained from breaking his legs. This also fulfilled Scripture: "not a bone of him shall be broken" (19:36, from Ps. 34:20; see also Exod. 12:46; Num. 9:12). Instead of breaking his bones, one of the soldiers pierced his side, from which blood and water then issued. This also fulfilled prophecy: "They will look to him whom they pierced" (19:37, from Zech. 12:10).

All happened as it was supposed to happen. No one but Jesus, however, was aware of this. Since he knew his destiny (see 18:37), he walked into death boldly and courageously. He walked into death as the Son of God. According to John's narrative, there is no scene of agony in the Garden of Gethsemane and there is no crying out "My God, My God, why have you forsaken me" on the cross. The other Gospels show us Jesus' human side. They describe the sufferings of the man who would become our sympathetic high priest. John shows us the God-man. He is the man in whom Pilate could find no fault. He is the man who, while dying on the cross, showed his concern for the well-being of his mother. He is the man who laid down his life on his own accord. When it was all finished, Jesus, of his own volition, gave up his spirit. As was foretold, no one took his life from him. He had authority to give it up and then retake it.

John, as with the other Gospel writers, does not give any details about the crucifixion process; he simply says "they crucified him." We later discover that Jesus' hands must have been nailed to the cross (see 20:25, 27). We are told, however, that a placard was placed on the cross, which read "JESUS THE NAZARENE, THE KING OF THE JEWS." While the chief priests would have wanted Jesus' crime posted as a false claim to kingship (19:22), Pilate provided a tribute to Jesus' kingship in a trilingual placard that everyone in Palestine could read, for it was written in the three major languages of the day: Hebrew (or, Aramaic—the language of the Jews), Latin (the Roman language, the official language), and Greek (the lingua franca, the common tongue). The universalism of this placard affirmed Jesus' own prediction concerning the universal effect of his death, for he prophesied that his crucifixion would become the one force that drew all people to himself (see 12:32; cf. 11:51–52). Knowing that he accomplished the Father's will, Jesus proclaimed with his dying breath, *tetelestai* ("it is finished")! This expression can also mean, "it is accomplished," "it is fulfilled," or even, "it is paid in full."[1] His death accomplished redemption—"paid in full"— and his death fulfilled all the Old Testament prophecies.

Four women witnessed Jesus' crucifixion: Jesus' mother, the sister of his mother, Mary the wife of Clopas, and Mary Magdalene. In contrast to the four soldiers who had no regard for Jesus, these women, as devoted followers, must have been overwhelmed with grief as they watched their Lord die. John, the beloved one, also stood by the cross. He made a point of saying that he saw the soldiers pierce Jesus with a lance and witnessed the blood and water flowing from his side. The account of Christ's crucifixion is to be trusted because it was written by an eyewitness.[2]

Excursus: The Significance of Christ's Crucifixion

The crucifixion of God's Son was God's paramount display of his love to humankind. This is evident to most believers. But many may not see that the crucifixion equally manifested the Son's love for the Father. The Scripture tells us that the Son was willing to go to the cross because he loved the Father (John 14:31). The Son must have known that this would be his destiny when the Godhead first decided to create man—for it must have been foreknown that man would need redemption. The Bible says that Christ, as the Lamb of God, was foreordained to crucifixion (1 Pet. 1:19–20). His death on the cross was not an afterthought or merely a remedy; it was the fulfillment of the determined counsel and foreknowledge of God (Acts 2:23). Thus, the Scripture can speak of "the Lamb slain from the foundation of the world" (Rev. 13:8).[3]

Some of the Old Testament believers anticipated the coming of the Messiah (see John 8:56; Heb. 11); it would be a day when the Savior's blood would pay the price for their redemption. The blood of bulls and goats served as an earnest until the actual payment was made (Rom. 3:25). Having covered their sins, God was anxious to have his people approach him for worship and fellowship, but most of the Israelites were reluctant to approach him.

His visitations incited fear rather than love. As much as God may have wanted to approach his people and manifest his love to them, the people shrank back and cowered with trembling when God would draw near (see Exod. 21; Heb. 12:18–21). In fact, while God was drawing near, the Israelites were falling away into idolatry. This frustrated love affair characterizes the Old Testament narrative. God's love for his people was rarely reciprocated and frequently slighted. How often God lamented Israel's idolatrous harlotry! No matter what God did to attract his people to himself, they were unenchanted. He approached them again and again; he wooed them and warned them. He loved them but they (as a whole) had little or no love for him. Something had to be done if God wanted to attract people to himself.

When the time was ripe, God sent forth his beloved Son into the world to die on the cross. The Son would pay the price for man's redemption. But God's great act of sending his Son to die on the cross was done not only for the sake of accomplishing a legal redemption; it was done for the purpose of demonstrating God's ultimate love for humankind (see Rom. 5:8). God went all the way— to the extent of sacrificing his own Son—to show how much he loved us. Mysteriously, the cross of Christ became the attracting force, drawing people's hearts to God like a great magnet.

Most people are not brought to salvation by understanding the legal ramifications of redemption; they are saved, experientially, by the profound and compelling display of God's love as manifested in the crucified Jesus. Millions have been drawn to God by the constraining power manifested in Christ's cross. Paul, as if speaking for all of us who have known that love, exclaimed, "For the love of Christ constrains me. Because we thus judge, if one died for all, then all died. And he died for all, that those who live might no longer live for themselves but for him who for their sake died and was raised" (2 Cor. 5:14–15).

Redemption could not have been accomplished if God had not partaken of flesh and blood—mortality. God cannot die because he is immortal; he had to partake of actual humanity in order to participate in mortality. The Son of God, out of love for his Father, willingly relinquished his equality with the Father to become subservient to him for the purpose of accomplishing redemption. He was sent by the Father to experience incarnation, human living, and crucifixion. This was quite a "humbling," an "emptying-out" (in Greek called *kenosis*—"the process of emptying") of his divine prerogatives and equalities with the Father (see Phil. 2:5–11). The Son did it because he loved the Father.

All the time he was on earth, Jesus must have longed to return to the Father and so recapture that special fellowship and communion he had enjoyed with the Father. (Of course, in his return to the Father he, as a man, even the God-man, would be joining him, having taken the lead for all the sons of God yet to come.) It must have been difficult for the Son to leave that divine, eternal communion in order to join the human race. We believers must thank him for that sacrifice of love. He paved the way for us to have access to God; he restored the fellowship between God and man. We, who had been alienated from God due to the fall, can now return to God our Father. He foreknew the fall and he foresaw the need for redemption and salvation. Even more, he foreknew and predestined all those who would come to believe in his Son. Not only was the Lamb's destiny foreordained, so was our salvation.

Rising from the Dead

John 19:38–20:29

ike all human beings, Jesus was buried after his death; unlike all other mortals, he rose from the grave never to die again. After his burial and resurrection, Jesus generated the new creation by breathing his Spirit into the disciples and thereby fulfilled all that he had promised them. This is the consummation of Jesus' journey and the germination of the disciples' spiritual peregrination.

Resurrection and regeneration are closely linked in the Scriptures—in the same way that crucifixion and redemption form an inseparable unity. As redemption was not possible without Christ's crucifixion, so regeneration is not possible without Christ's resurrection. The Scripture plainly says that we have been born again through the resurrection of Christ (1 Pet. 1:23).

After Christ was raised from the dead, he called the disciples his brothers (Matt. 28:10; John 20:17) and declared that his God was now their God, and his Father their Father. Through resurrection, the disciples had become the brothers of Jesus, possessing the same divine life and the same Father. As "the firstborn from among the dead" (Col. 1:18; Rev. 1:15), Jesus Christ became "the firstborn among many brothers" (Rom. 8:29).

We cannot ever fully understand what happened when Christ arose from the dead, but the topic is worth our investigation because we owe our Christian origination to Christ's resurrection. The resurrection is our "roots"—not just in the sense of "origin" but also in the sense of "life-supply." Because Christ lives, we live; and we continue to live our spiritual lives dependent on him, the risen One.

Jesus' Burial (19:38–42)

Two men, both secret disciples of Jesus, came forward to take care of Jesus' burial. They both had feared persecution from the Jewish religious leaders, so they had not openly followed Jesus (see 7:13; 12:42–43). This is clearly indicated in John's description of the first man: "Joseph of Arimathea (being a disciple of Jesus, but a secret one, for fear of the Jewish leaders)." When Joseph asked Pilate if he could take Jesus' body to give him proper burial, Pilate assented. The other secret disciple was Nicodemus, who is identified for John's readers as the "one who at first came to him [Jesus] by night" (see 3:1–21; cf. 7:50–52).

Nicodemus joined wealthy Joseph of Arimathea (cf. Matt. 27:57) in embalming and wrapping Jesus' body in regal style. Nicodemus' actions demonstrated that he considered Jesus worthy of a king's burial. He used an extraordinarily large amount of burial unguent (75 pounds), which must have cost Nicodemus a great sum. Such a lavish amount of ointment was offered only to kings at the time of burial. Both men then "took Jesus' body and bound it in fine linen with the spices, as is the burial custom of the Jews" (19:40). Unlike the Egyptians who used spices in the embalming process, Jews used spices as an aromatic to stifle the smell of putrification.

Joseph demonstrated his affection for Jesus by giving his own tomb for Jesus' burial (see Matt. 27:60). Such tombs, hewn out of the solid rock and closed with heavy stones, were expensive. It was fortuitous that Joseph had a tomb nearby and that he wanted to put Jesus' body there because the burial had to happen quickly—prior to the coming of the Sabbath, which began at sunset on Friday, which is here called "the Jewish day of preparation."

Jesus' Resurrection (20:1–29)

In John 12:1–8 we saw how one woman, Mary the sister of Lazarus, demonstrated her affection for Jesus. John 20:1–18 spotlights another woman, Mary Magdalene, who also exhibited her affection for her Master. The first Mary anointed Jesus before his death; the second Mary came to anoint him after his death. Both women loved Jesus.

Mary Magdalene had followed Jesus to the cross, watched his crucifixion, and then remained to see where he was buried (see Matt. 27:61). His death broke her heart. After Jesus' burial she came at the break of dawn on the first day of the week to the tomb. When she arrived and saw the stone removed, she surmised that someone had taken away her Lord. After she reported this to the disciples, John and Peter ran to the tomb. Both looked in and saw that it was empty. Then the narrative says that John believed (20:8). Since there is no direct object after "believed," the reader has to imagine what John believed. The simplest explanation is that John believed Mary's story about the empty tomb; however, it could very well be that John believed in Jesus' resurrection. If the latter meaning was intended, we must understand the next verse (v. 9) to indicate that, though John had come to believe in Jesus' resurrection, he had not yet known the Scripture about the resurrection (see note on 2:22). He had faith but no knowledge; the knowledge would come later and affirm the faith.

After John and Peter returned home, Mary remained outside the tomb weeping. Then she stooped down and looked into the tomb and saw two angels—one at the feet and the other at the head of where Jesus had laid. When the angels asked her why she was weeping, she expressed her obsession: "they took away my Lord." She turned around—no doubt to seek him—and there he was. But she did not recognize him. Imagining him to be the gardener, she blurted out: "Tell me where you placed him." His familiar voice, calling her "Mary," brought her to her senses. Having found him, Mary clung to him. But Jesus told her, "Stop clinging to me." The Greek verb underlying "clinging" is a present imperative. The action had already begun when Jesus told Mary, "Stop clinging to me." He was not preventing Mary from touching him (which would be the meaning if an aorist imperative had been used).

Mary wanted to hold onto Jesus and so reinstate her former relationship with him, but Jesus, via resurrection, had entered into a new state of being and a new sphere of living. Mary could no longer know him according to the old way. Second Corinthians 5:16–17 indicates that we should no longer know Christ according to the flesh (i.e., according to his human existence) because old things have passed away and all things have become new.

Jesus affirmed this new change when he told Mary, "Go to my *brothers* and tell them, I am ascending to My Father and *your* Father, and My God and *your* God." Because of Christ's resurrection, his disciples had now become Jesus' brothers (see also Matt. 28:10). Resurrection creates this new relationship because it provides for the regeneration of every believer. First Peter 1:3 says that we have been born again to a new hope through the resurrection of Jesus from the dead. As possessors of the divine life (see Eph. 4:18) and partakers of the divine nature (2 Pet. 1:4), all the believers have become Jesus' brothers, having the same God and the same Father!

Jesus told Mary, "I am ascending to My Father." The language gives no indication that this ascension would be in the future. We must be careful not to superimpose a timetable upon John's Gospel that is not indigenous to John's narrative. According to John's chronology, the Lord would arise from the dead, ascend to the Father, and then come to the disciples—all within "a little while" (see 14:2–3, 18–20, 23; 16:16–22 and the comments on these verses). All this happens within the confines of John's Gospel. The ascension spoken of in Luke 24:51 and Acts 1:9 is another ascension that occurred after the forty-day period of Jesus' resurrection appearances (Acts 1:3).

Jesus met Mary on the morning of the resurrection. On the very same evening Jesus made his first appearance to his disciples. This appearance is astounding because Jesus penetrated the closed room and manifested himself in their midst. He could do this because resurrection and the subsequent glorification had altered his form. In resurrection, he had become life-giving spirit (1 Cor. 15:42–45). At the same time, he still retained his humanity—but a glorified one. In resurrection, he was the same person in a different form (see Mark 16:12). In this new spiritual form, he was able to transcend all physical barriers. He was able to penetrate matter and even penetrate human beings. The risen Christ, as spirit and as one with the Holy Spirit, is able to enter into people and indwell them. At the same time, he retains his distinct human existence in heaven at God's right hand. It is an amazing mystery.

On the evening of his resurrection, Jesus appeared to his disciples and showed them his hands and side. They thought they were being visited by a ghost or phantom (see Luke 24:37–39). His physical appearance reassured them that it was Jesus himself in their midst. Jesus graced them with his peace and then commissioned them just as he had been commissioned by the Father. The disciples were to be his ongoing testimony, even as he had been the Father's. As the Father sent the Son, so the Son now sends the apostles. But before doing so, he imparted the Holy Spirit into them.

The impartation of the Holy Spirit was accomplished by Jesus breathing the Holy Spirit into his disciples: "he breathed into them and said, 'Receive the Holy Spirit'" (20:22). In a sense this verse consummates the Gospel of John because the Spirit who had been promised in 7:37–39; 14:16–20, 26; 15:26; and 16:7–15 is now at last given to the disciples. After the Lord commissioned the disciples, he breathed *(enephusēsen)* into them and said, "Receive Holy Spirit." Jesus' breathing into them recapitulates God's breathing into Adam (see Gen. 2:7, LXX, where *enephusēsen* is used), and thus denotes that Jesus' infusion inspired a new genesis, in which he regenerated the disciples (see 1 Pet. 1:3). With this "inbreathing" came the actual impartation of the promised Holy Spirit.

This impartation was not a symbolic act or a mere prefigure of the Pentecostal outpouring. Some commentators and translators, however, have asserted that since the Greek reads *pneuma hagion* (anarthrous), it does not designate the personal Holy Spirit but rather an earnest of that gift or an affusion of the Spirit.[1] But the expression *pneuma hagion,* appearing eighty-six times in the New Testament, is used thirty-seven times with an article and forty-nine times without an article! Whether arthrous or anarthrous, *pneuma hagion* designates the unique Holy Spirit.

The real reason some insist on saying that the John 20:22 infusion was either a symbolic act or a foretaste is they believe that the Holy Spirit was given only at Pentecost and not until then. For example, J. B. Phillips translated that last part of the verse as, "Receive holy spirit"—to which he appended a note, "Lit. 'receive holy spirit.' Historically the Holy Spirit was not given until Pentecost."[2] But the Gospel of John doesn't fit this schema, for it has its own chronology. According to the entire context of John's Gospel, the Lord Jesus would first ascend to the Father and then come to the disciples to give them the promised Spirit. John's Gospel, as a self-contained unit, has its own time frame. Because the timing does not coincide with the Luke–Acts sequence does not mean it is invalid, nor do the two accounts contradict each other. The apostles receive the Spirit into them on the evening of the resurrection, and the Spirit came upon them on the day of Pentecost. They were infilled and endued with the same Spirit.

But one of the disciples, Thomas, missed the meeting. When the disciples told him that Jesus had appeared to them, he did not believe. He insisted that he see Jesus with his eyes and touch Jesus' wounds with his hands. At their next meeting, eight days later, Thomas was present when Jesus appeared again. Jesus used Thomas' very own words about having to see the wounds in Jesus' hands and side before he would believe. How could Jesus have known what Thomas had said if Jesus was still dead? In an instant, Thomas must have realized that Jesus, in his invisible presence, was there when he (Thomas) had voiced his doubts to the other disciples. Thomas must have realized that Jesus, as God, sees all, hears all, knows all. Thus, he exclaimed to Jesus, "My Lord and my God!" Thomas' exclamation is one of the clearest affirmations of Jesus' deity in the New Testament (see also John 1:1, 18; 8:58; 10:30; Rom. 9:5; Phil. 2:6; Col. 2:9; Titus 2:13; 2 Pet. 1:1; 1 John 5:20). Though Thomas hailed Jesus as his Lord and God, Jesus reproved Thomas' way of faith—for he first saw and then believed. The blessed ones are those who don't see and yet believe. This blessing would be effective for the millions of Christians who have never seen Jesus yet believe in him (see 2 Cor. 5:7; 1 Pet. 1:8).

Excursus: The Significance of Christ's Resurrection

Few Christians have a thorough understanding of Christ's resurrection. They may understand his rising from the dead, but they may not grasp the significance of resurrection. Several people were raised from the dead, as recorded in the Bible. The widow's son was raised by Elijah, another widow's son was raised by Jesus, and Lazarus was raised by Jesus. However, their revitalization (or resuscitation) is absolutely not the same as Christ's resurrection. They arose only to die again; he arose to live forever more. They arose still doomed by corruptibility; he arose incorruptible. They arose with no change to their constitution; he arose in a significantly different form.

When Jesus arose, three significant things happened to him. He was glorified, was transfigured, and became spirit. All three happened simultaneously. When he was resurrected, he was glorified (see Luke 24:26). At the same time, his body was transfigured into a glorious one (Phil. 3:21). Equally so—and quite mysteriously—he became life-giving spirit (1 Cor. 15:45).

Prior to the Lord's crucifixion and resurrection he declared, "The hour has come for the Son of Man to be glorified. Truly, truly, I say unto you, unless a grain of wheat falls into the ground and dies, it abides alone; but if it dies, it brings forth many grains" (John 12:23–24). This declaration provides the best picture of resurrection. Paul also used this illustration. He likened the resurrection glory to a grain being sown in death, then coming forth in life. Actually, Paul used this illustration when answering two questions the Corinthians posed about resurrection: How are the dead raised? With what sort of body do they come? (1 Cor. 15:35).

To the first question Paul responded, "Foolish man, what you sow is not made alive unless it dies" (15:36). This follows perfectly the Lord's saying in John 12:24, and the two mutually explain each other. The grain must die before it can be quickened. Paul devotes more explanation to the second question, and the Spirit inspired his sublime utterance to unfold this mystery. Using the same natural example of the grain of wheat, Paul revealed that the body that comes forth in resurrection is altogether different in form from that which had been sown. Through an organic process, the single bare grain is transformed into a stalk of wheat. In essence, the grain and the stalk are one and the same—the latter simply being the living growth and expressed expansion of the former. In short, the stalk is the glory of the grain or, the glorified grain. This illustration shows that Jesus' resurrected body was altogether different from the one that was buried. In death, he had been sown in corruption, dishonor, and weakness; but in resurrection, he came forth in incorruption, glory, and power. The natural body that Jesus possessed as a man became a spiritual body. And at the same time Christ became "life-giving spirit." The first man, Adam, became a living soul with a "soulical body";[3] the last Adam, Jesus, became life-giving spirit with a spiritual body (1 Cor. 15:44–45).

Jesus became life-giving spirit. Notice the verse does not say Jesus became the Spirit—as if the second person of the Trinity became the third, but that Jesus became spirit in the sense that his mortal existence and form were metamorphosed into a spiritual existence and form. Jesus' person was not changed through the resurrection, only his form. With this changed spiritual form, Jesus regained the essential state of being he had emptied himself of in becoming a man. Before he became a man, he subsisted in the form of God (Phil. 2:6), which form is Spirit and thereby was united to the Spirit (the third of the Trinity), while still remaining distinct. The Scriptures assert this twofold relationship. On one hand, there are numerous verses that certify the fact that the Spirit and Jesus are united: "the Lord is the Spirit" (2 Cor. 3:17); "the Lord, who is Spirit" (2 Cor. 3:18); "the Spirit of Christ" (Rom. 8:9); "the Spirit of Jesus Christ" (Phil. 1:19); and "the Spirit of his Son" (Gal. 4:6). On the other hand, there are many Scriptures that substantiate the truth that the Son and the Spirit are distinct: "I [the Son] will send you another Comforter, the Spirit of truth" (John 15:26); "having received from the Father the promise of the Holy Spirit, he [Jesus] has poured forth this" (Acts 2:33); "for through him [the Son], we both have our access in one Spirit to the Father" (Eph. 2:18).

All three "persons" of the Godhead are eternal, distinct, and unchangeable. One did not become the other: the Father did not become the Son, nor did the Son become the Spirit. The Triune God did not evolve from one mode to another—from Father to Son to Spirit. The three have always remained distinct yet one. Thus, when the Scripture says that the Lord "became life-giving spirit," it does not mean that the Son became the Holy Spirit. But it does indicate that Christ, via resurrection, appropriated a new, spiritual form (while still retaining a body—a glorified one) that enabled him to commence a new spiritual existence. First Peter 3:18 says that Jesus was "put to death in the flesh, quickened in the spirit." Commenting on this verse, Henry Alford wrote: "He the God-man Christ Jesus, body and soul, ceased to live in the flesh, began to live in the Spirit; ceased to live a fleshly mortal life, began to live a spiritual resurrection life."[4] With this new spiritual existence, Christ, as spirit and through the Holy Spirit, could indwell millions of believers simultaneously. Before the resurrection, Jesus was limited by his mortal body; after his resurrection, Jesus could be experienced without limit by all his believers. Before his resurrection, Christ could dwell only *among* his believers; after his resurrection, he could dwell *in* his believers. Because Christ became spirit through resurrection, he can be experienced by those he indwells. The Spirit of Christ now makes Christ very real and experiential. How good it is to have his Spirit! As a Christian, I have no other way to experience Christ but in, through, and as the Spirit. Prior to the resurrection the disciples could not experience Christ indwelling them because he was still a man limited by his human body. But after the resurrection there was a great change: Jesus' form changed so that he could then (and now) indwell the believers.

The Lord Jesus entered into a new kind of existence when he was raised from the dead because he was glorified and simultaneously became spirit—or, to coin a phrase, he was "pneumafied" (from the Greek word for "spirit," *pneuma*). It appears that when he arose, the indwelling Spirit penetrated and saturated his body so as to constitute his entire being with spirit. This is not my teaching alone; several noted Christian authors have advanced the same description of the Lord's resurrection. In fact, a great deal of study in the area of pneumatology (the study of the Spirit) points out that the risen Christ and the Spirit were united via Christ's resurrection.

William Milligan, the author of the best English classic on the subject of the resurrection, said that the risen Christ is spirit. In that classic, called *The Resurrection of Our Lord,* he wrote the following:

> The condition of our Lord after his Resurrection was viewed by the sacred writers as essentially a state of *pneuma* (spirit). Not indeed that our Lord had then no body, for it is the constant lesson of Scripture that a body was possessed by him; but that the deepest, the fundamental characteristic of his state, interpenetrating even the body, and moulding it into a complete adaptation to and harmony with his spirit, was *pneuma*. In other words, it is proposed to inquire whether the word *pneuma* in the New Testament is not used as a short description of what our Lord was after his Resurrection, in contrast with what he was during the days of his humiliation upon earth.[5]

Milligan went on from there to show that several Scriptures affirm that the resurrected Christ is spirit. He cited 1 Corinthians 6:17 to show that the believer who is joined with the risen Lord must be joined to him as spirit because he who is joined to the Lord is said to be "one spirit" with him. He used 2 Corinthians 3:17–18 to demonstrate that the Lord who is the Spirit is none other than the risen Christ. He also employed 1 Timothy 3:16; Romans 1:3–4; and Hebrews 9:14 to prove that the risen Lord is spirit.[6] Henry Alford, commenting on Hebrews 9:14, related that the divine personality in Christ in the resurrection so completely ruled and absorbed his flesh that Paul so spoke of him in 1 Corinthians 15:45 as life-giving Spirit and in 2 Corinthians 3:17 as the Spirit.[7] And note the remarks of Richard Gaffin, a contemporary author, who wrote concerning the resurrection of Christ:

> Christ (as incarnate) experiences a spiritual qualification and transformation so thorough, and endowment with the Spirit so complete that as a result they can now be equated. This unprecedented possession of the Spirit and the accompanying change in Christ result in a unity so close that not only can it be said simply that the Spirit makes alive, but also that Christ as Spirit makes alive.[8]

When we read the last chapters of the Gospels, we realize that a great change had transpired in our Lord after the resurrection. By entering into glory he had entered into a new sphere of existence. At one moment he was visible; in another he became invisible (Luke 24:31). He was defying the limitations of space and perhaps even time. In the early morning of the day of resurrection, he appeared to Mary Magdalene in the garden (John 20:11–17), then to some of the other women (Matt. 28:9). After this, he ascended to his Father (John 20:17). Then he returned to appear to Peter, who had gone home (Luke 24:34; John 20:10). On the same day, in the late afternoon, he took a seven-mile walk with two disciples on their way to Emmaus (Luke 24:13–33), following which he appeared to the disciples as they were assembled in a closed room somewhere in Jerusalem (Luke 24:33–48; John 20:19–23). It is nearly impossible to follow a sequential, chronological order of all these happenings. What Jesus did was humanly impossible. How could he make all of these appearances on the same day? All we can say is that resurrection greatly changed his sphere of existence. As spirit, and yet with a body—a glorified one—he was no longer limited by time and space.

Through resurrection, Jesus had acquired a different form (see Mark 16:12). As to his person, he was still the same Jesus who had walked in Galilee and was crucified at Calvary. His person had not changed. It never will, for it is immutable. But his form changed; he is now "life-giving spirit." This was the ultimate outcome of his spiritual journey—the consummation of his life on earth. To use a metaphor, the caterpillar had become a monarch butterfly—and Jesus was in full flight in his new liberated being, the spirit.

As spirit, Christ is now able to indwell all of his believers. This is precious. The same Jesus who walked in Galilee, was crucified at Calvary, and then arose is now in me! I do not have a representative in me, but the very Christ himself as life-giving spirit. I do not have an impersonal power in me or a mighty force; I have the glorified, resurrected Christ as spirit dwelling in me. A person is in me—and in all Christians! Through the believers, Jesus continues his journey.

21 The Conclusion and Epilogue to the Journey

John 20:30–21:25

Because the Gospel fittingly ends at 20:30–31, it is obvious that the twenty-first chapter is an epilogue. The question remains, however: Was the epilogue intrinsic to the original design of the Gospel, or was it added as an afterthought? It is possible that the first edition was published without an epilogue, and a second edition with an epilogue. If so, the two editions of John's Gospel may have circulated simultaneously until the first was superseded by the second, longer edition. The second edition, containing the epilogue, seems to be the work of the same person who composed the first edition. But there are various opinions about who wrote the twenty-first chapter. Some ascribe sole authorship to John, the son of Zebedee; others have attributed the epilogue to the coauthorship of John the apostle with certain members of the Johannine community, such as the Ephesian elders (this was the view of Clement of Alexandria and the Muratorian Canon); others, to certain members of the Johannine community who composed it after the death of the beloved disciple; and others (who do not espouse Johannine authorship of any part of the Gospel), to the same writer who composed the first twenty chapters.

I think it is quite likely that John the apostle wrote the first twenty chapters, then later in his life, with the assistance of certain members of his community, he appended another chapter, wherein he clarified the rumor that he would not die before the Lord's return (21:22–23). And I think it is possible that the early papyrus manuscripts, P5 and P75, provide textual evidence of the earliest edition before it was superseded by the second edition—if both, in fact, originally contained only twenty chapters each.[1]

In any event, this epilogue records Jesus' appearance to the disciples beside the Sea of Tiberias in Galilee. Jesus had made at least six appearances in (or around) Jerusalem: to Mary Magdalene (Mark 16:9–11; John 20:11–18), to the other women (Matt. 28:8–10; Mark 16:8; Luke 24:9–11), to Peter (Luke 24:34; 1 Cor. 15:5), to two disciples (Luke 24:36–49; John 20:19–23), and to the disciples with Thomas (John 20:24–29). After the Jerusalem appearances, the disciples evidently returned to Galilee. Jesus made more appearances there: to the disciples on a mountain in Galilee (Matt. 28:16–20; Mark 16:15–18); to five hundred believers (1 Cor. 15:6); to James, his brother (1 Cor. 15:7), and to the seven disciples who went fishing on the Sea of Tiberias. Prior to his resurrection, Jesus had told his disciples that he would meet them at an appointed place in Galilee after he arose from the dead (see Mark 14:28). But due to their unbelief and fear, they remained in Jerusalem. So Jesus first appeared to them in Jerusalem and then in Galilee.

The Galilean appearances were important for restoring former disciples to a renewed faith in Jesus. Only twelve disciples had followed Jesus all the way to his final journey to Jerusalem. In fact, several disciples had left Jesus midway into his ministry (see John 6:60–66). It is quite likely that his Galilean appearances revived these disciples—and there were perhaps as many as five hundred who stayed behind in Galilee. The Galilean resurrection appearances were also used by Jesus to affirm the eleven apostles. In the appearance recorded in John 21, Jesus reinstated Peter as a leader and example for the flock and affirmed John, the author of the Gospel.

The First Conclusion (20:30–31)

Since an appended epilogue follows, these two verses appear to be John's first conclusion to his book. As in Luke's preface (Luke 1:1–4), the purpose of these two verses is to tell us why John wrote this Gospel: "There are many other signs, then, that Jesus did before his disciples, which have not been written in this book; but these have been written that you may continue to believe that Jesus is the Christ, the Son of God, and that by believing you may have life in his name."

This Gospel's raison d'être is very clear. To have read this Gospel and not believed that Jesus is the Christ, the Son of God, is to have missed John's purpose for writing it. This Gospel is focused on the person, Jesus. He is the Christ, the Son of God, who came to give life to those who believe in his name (i.e., his identity).

Quite significantly, John wrote this Gospel primarily to encourage those who already believed to continue in their faith. This can be inferred because John used the present tense for the subjunctive verb *pisteuō,* rather than the aorist. The aorist would have indicated initial belief, but the present indicates continual belief.[2] If indeed John intended this Gospel to go to those who already believed, we can understand why this Gospel has so much more theological, spiritual, and experiential depth than the Synoptic Gospels. Without detracting from the other Gospels, it is generally admitted that John's is the most profound. At the same time, it is the most simple. New believers benefit from it, and so do the most mature.

The Epilogue (21:1–23)

It was natural for some of the disciples to return to their old occupation, fishing, once they had returned to Galilee. Peter took the lead, and six other disciples went with him. That night, however, they caught nothing. Perhaps this was a déjà vu experience for Peter. Just before the Lord appeared to Peter the first time, Peter had been out fishing, catching nothing. Peter might have been reminiscing about that first miraculous draught. That miracle caused Peter to fall on his knees and ask Jesus to depart from him, a sinful man (see Luke 5:1–11). Here he was again, fishing, catching nothing, lacking the presence of the Lord.

Little did Peter know that Jesus was standing on the shore, waiting for the coming of dawn, after which he would make another appearance to the disciples, especially for Peter's sake. The repeated miraculous draught of fish was particularly intended to affect Peter. It did. Peter did not say a word as he dragged the net full of fish to shore and then (with the other disciples) ate the break-fast Jesus had prepared even before they caught the fish.

This third manifestation of the Lord had a profound effect on the disciples. His presence silenced them, humbled them, and rein-stated them. It seems that their going fishing was a kind of diver-sion from their commission, or, at worst, a kind of backsliding to the former things. In this appearance, Jesus brought them into line with his purposes, for he specifically exhorted Peter to take care of shepherding the flock.

After breakfast Jesus asked Peter, "Do you love me more than these men do?" (21:15). According to the Greek, this could also be rendered, "Do you love me more than these things?" (i.e., the fish, the boat, and all things related to the fishing occupation). Both ren-derings are compatible with the context, but in light of the fact that Peter had claimed, in the presence of all the disciples, that he would never forsake the Lord, even if all the others did (see Matt. 26:33; Mark 14:29; John 13:37), it seems that Jesus was exposing Peter for having thought he loved him more than the other disciples did.

Three times Jesus asked Peter if he loved him (21:15–17). The first two times Jesus used the word *agapaō* and the last time *phileō* to express two different kinds of love. In all three of his responses, Peter used the word *phileō*. The Greek word *agapaō* designates the most noble action of love, for this word indicates volitional, respon-sible love, love that emanates not so much from the emotion as from the rational soul. The Greek word *phileō* designates the action of love that emanates from liking someone or something. It con-veys the idea of fondness.[3] Peter, quite honestly, told Jesus that he was fond of him. Peter could not say that he had demonstrated *agapē* love. In fact, he had failed to exercise self-sacrificial love at the time of Jesus' trial. Three times Peter denied him; three times Jesus asked Peter if he loved him. The third time, stooping to Peter's level, Jesus asked Peter if he was fond of him. Peter told him what he already knew: "I am fond of you."

Each time Peter told Jesus "I am fond of you," Jesus exhorted Peter to care for his precious lambs ("young lambs" and "little sheep" are terms of endearment). Peter was charged to care for them by feeding and shepherding them. Peter never forgot this charge; he became a devoted shepherd of the flock (see 1 Pet. 5:1–4). But he would pay the price for this devotion. He, like the good Shepherd, would be led to the cross. Jesus told him, "When you were younger, you used to gird yourself and go where you wanted; but when you grow old, you will stretch out your hands, and someone else will gird you, and take you where you do not want to go" (21:18). On the surface, this seems to depict what happens to an older man who must become dependent upon others. But John's explanation dispels this notion: "this he said, signifying with what kind of death he would glorify God" (21:19). The image depicts Peter's death by crucifixion. Tertullian (ca. A.D. 212), referring to John 21:18, said that Peter was "girded by another" when his arms were stretched out and fastened to the cross. Once Jesus told him this, Peter knew what death lay before him. This prophecy remained with Peter all his days (see 2 Pet. 1:14).

Having been told of his destiny, Peter wanted to know what would happen to John. Jesus' response is somewhat mystifying: "If I want him to remain until I come, what is that to you?" Apparently, this statement could mean that John would remain alive on earth until the coming of the Lord (i.e., until the parousia). Quite obviously, that is exactly how some of John's contemporaries understood the statement. For they instigated a saying among the brothers that John would not die. (For if John remained alive until the Lord's coming, he would never have to experience death.)

Some commentators think that John had died by the time the epilogue was written and therefore someone else wrote the epilogue to clear up the church's misconception about the timing of Jesus' parousia. But if John "had died by then, it would have been easy to refute the unfounded report by showing how it had been falsified by the event."[4] Thus, it is John himself who took the initiative to make the clarification while he was still alive so that the believers would not think that Jesus would return before John died. In essence, Jesus said that John *could* stay alive until his coming (if the Lord so willed), not that John *would* stay alive until his coming. The Lord's sovereignty over each person's life was the issue, not the duration of John's life. Each person is responsible to follow the Lord according to what the Lord has revealed. The command is clear: "you follow me" (21:22). What Jesus was communicating to Peter was that Peter should not be concerned about what would become of John's life; rather, Peter was responsible to follow the Lord according to what the Lord had revealed to him, and John likewise.[5]

The Colophon (21:24–25)

The last two verses of the Gospel contain the colophon that attests to the veracity of John's written testimony. Here the writer identifies himself with the disciple mentioned in the above narrative, whom I consider to be John, the son of Zebedee. John's testimony is trustworthy because he was that disciple whom Jesus loved and that disciple who was an eyewitness of Jesus' life and ministry. The statement "we know that his testimony is true" is the attestation of some of John's contemporaries who knew that what John wrote was true. Some scholars think these contemporaries were the Ephesian elders. (John resided in Ephesus in his later years.) Westcott wrote, "The words were probably added by the Ephesian elders, to whom the preceding narrative had been given both orally and in writing."[6]

John concludes his Gospel with the grand statement, "And there are many other things that Jesus did, which if they were written in detail [lit. one by one], I suppose that even the world itself could not contain the books that would be written." This final statement is an honest admission that his book was far from being exhaustive, because he recorded only some of the things Jesus did. Not enough could be said about what Jesus did. Even if the whole world were a library, it could not contain all books that could be written about Jesus because every single thing he did was worth a sermon. John had selected only certain events and expanded each one into a vignette depicting a significant phase of Jesus' living journey. What is important to note is that John considered his Gospel to be "a book"—a work of literature—not just notes or a memoir. He had crafted a literary work that captured the essence of Jesus' life and many moments in the most significant journey that ever occurred on earth. John was privileged to have seen this God-man live and move among them, and we are privileged to read his inspired account.

Postscript

Thoughts for Our Spiritual Journey

The spiritual journey that is presented in John's Gospel is a theme that weaves its way throughout the whole New Testament. This theme is especially prominent in the epistles—primarily Romans, 1 Corinthians, Hebrews, 1 Peter, and 1 John. In all of these writings, there is journey imagery and journey movement. Christians are encouraged to move on in their spiritual journey: to remain steadfast to the end, to reach full spiritual maturity, to be like Christ when we meet him at the end of the road. Thus, these epistles carry forward the journey that was begun in John. The consummation of the journey is depicted in the final chapters of the last book of the Bible. In Revelation, we see the journey's end and the eternal delights that follow.

A Journey to Full Maturity

Once we have been born again by the Spirit of Jesus Christ, we become children of God—born of God's divine nature. Our regeneration gives us everything we need for our Christian lives, but we need an entire lifetime to discover what we have been given and to grow into mature sons and daughters of God. This process of maturation is often depicted in the Bible as a pathway on which every believer must traverse until he or she reaches the goal: conformation to the glorious image of God's Son. This is the goal toward which we press and the goal on which we fix our thoughts.

In the end, we will be like him—and we will see him as he is (1 John 3:2).

Jesus has not left us to reach this goal by our own efforts. If he did, none of us would ever make it. He has paved the way for us and even now is helping us get there. As the firstborn from among the dead (Col. 1:18; Rev. 1:5), Jesus became the firstborn among many brothers (Rom. 8:29). That makes Jesus our older brother. Now God has many sons and Jesus has many brothers. If the Son of God had not become man, died on the cross, and then arisen, this could not have been a reality. But it is a reality because the Son of God, as man, took the lead in accomplishing the heart's desire of God. God wanted many sons from among the human race; the Son of God, therefore, joined the human race to become the first man to be God's son. I know this sounds extraordinary, but it is true.

The second chapter of Hebrews tells us that the Son of God became a man in order to participate in our humanity, to feel our sufferings, and even to taste death on our behalf. In so doing, he became the pioneer, the captain of our salvation. He, as man, pioneered the way for all the other sons to follow. He, who was the express image of God's substance and the effulgence of his glory (Heb. 1:3), relinquished that place of glory and took a human body for the sake of accomplishing the Father's will. In that body he would suffer and die for our salvation (see Heb. 10:5–10). He did this because he loved the Father and because he anticipated the joy set before him (Heb. 12:2). His joy would be to return—via resurrection and ascension—to his Father. He would again be in glory, but now as a man!

As a man in glory, even as the glorified God-man, he is the one who pioneered the way for all other men to follow. Hebrews 2:10 calls him "the captain of our salvation," or this could as easily be rendered "the pioneer of our salvation" or "the leader of our salvation." The Greek word underlying "captain," "pioneer," and/or "leader" designates "the first one to lead the way" (*archēgon*, from *archē* [the first] and *agō* [to lead]). Hebrews 2:10 tells us that this Leader is the one who is leading many sons into glory.[1]

After Jesus himself entered into glory, he did not just stay there, awaiting our arrival. No, after having entered into glory, he came back to the many sons so as to be in their midst and then lead them into glory. The verses following Hebrews 2:10 tell us that Jesus is in the midst of the church; he is dwelling with all those whom he is not ashamed to call his brothers. It is impossible for our finite minds to comprehend how Jesus can both be on the throne in heaven and in the midst of the church simultaneously. But it is the truth—verified by the Scriptures and by our experience. Before Jesus left this world to return to the Father, he repeatedly told the disciples that he himself would be with them: "For where two or three are gathered together in my name, there am I in their midst" (Matt. 18:20); "Lo, I am with you always, even until the completion of the age" (Matt. 28:20); "I will not leave you orphans; I am coming to you" (John 14:18).

Jesus, the one in our midst, is leading us to where he has already gone—into the glorious presence of the Father. The path to that glorious destiny cannot be different than the one the Lord himself traversed. He left a pattern for us to follow, a mold for us to be conformed to. Each believer, if he or she is to grow and mature, must be conformed to the image of God's Son. The Father wills it because he desires all his children to reach maturity and so bear the image of the Beloved. To achieve his intention God works both inwardly and outwardly on each of his sons. The Bible calls the inward process "transformation" and the outward process "conformation."

Transformation involves an inward, metabolic-like renewal of our mind through which our inner man is changed into the likeness of Christ. Paul told the Roman believers: "Be transformed by the renewing of your minds" (Rom. 12:2). As our Christian life progresses, we should gradually notice that our thought-life is being changed from Christlessness to Christ-likeness. Transformation does not happen overnight—regeneration is instantaneous but not transformation. We are transformed to Christ's image gradually as we spend time beholding him in intimate fellowship. Eventually, we will begin to mirror the one we behold. Paul said, "We all with unveiled faces, mirroring the glory of the Lord, are being transformed into the same image, from one degree of glory to another, even as from the Lord who is the Spirit" (2 Cor. 3:18). As we behold the Lord, who is now the indwelling Spirit, we begin to reflect his image. This does not come from conscious imitation but from enjoyable communion with our indwelling Lord. One day we shall see him as he really is, for we shall be like him (1 John 3:2).

Concurrent with the inward process of transformation, each maturing son must undergo conformation. There is no escape, for this was predetermined for every child of God:

> And we know that God is working all things together for good to those who love him, to those who are called according to his purpose. Because whom he foreknew he also predestined to be conformed to the image of his Son, that he might be the first born among many brothers; and whom he predestined, these he also called; and whom he called, these he also justified; and whom he justified, these he also glorified. (Rom. 8:28–30)

Since it was God's desire and plan to have many sons, each one would have to be conformed to the prototype, Jesus. This is the common destiny of all Christians. Our horizon has been marked out beforehand.[2] Note how the words "predestined," "called," "justified," and especially "glorified" in Romans 8:29–30 are in the past tense. That is because God, from his eternal perspective, sees this process as having been already completed. From God's perspective, we have been glorified already because he sees us like his Son. But still, in the reality of time, we must undergo the process of being conformed to the image of God's Son. God is working together all things in the lives of those who love him and are called according to his purpose. His goal is to conform each son to the image of his beloved Son.

A Journey of Suffering

When one continues to read the rest of Romans 8, it is quite evident that the "things" God uses to conform us involve various kinds of suffering. Conformity to the image of Jesus Christ necessitates conformity to his death (see Phil. 3:10). Whereas transformation involves an inward, life-imparted change in our essential constitution, conformation entails outward pressure that works the image of Christ into us. If we are to be made like him, we must have both. To know Jesus, as far as Paul was concerned, was to know both the power of his resurrection and the fellowship of his sufferings (Phil. 3:10). No one likes to suffer; no one wants to be a Job. But Job was insightful when he said, "when he has tried me, I shall come forth as gold" (Job 23:10). Suffering produces an element in us that we do not inherently possess. God uses our sufferings to work the divine element into us, an element having an eternal weight of glory. As we cringe and complain, God works. It is a miserable process but it has a glorious end: we are conformed to the image of his Son.

The Lord Jesus left us a pattern, a pattern of suffering that cannot be avoided. This is the path that he, the pioneer of our salvation, took. The Father perfected him through sufferings (Heb. 2:10)—he, as a man, was made fully qualified to be our leader and even our merciful high priest because of what he suffered on our behalf. Christians should expect to suffer, at least in part, some of the things Jesus suffered. Of course, this does not mean that any of us can repeat his unique act of suffering on the cross for redemption. The annual reenactment of the crucifixion, as is practiced in some countries like the Philippines and Spain, is a travesty. His passion was complete, once and for all. We do, however, partake of other things that Jesus suffered.

Peter tells us that Jesus left "a pattern for us to follow in his steps" (1 Pet. 2:21). The Greek word underlying "pattern" *(hypogrammos)* in common Greek usage designated a tracing tablet that contained the entire Greek alphabet. Students would use this to trace the alphabet. They would have to learn each letter, from alpha to omega. The life of Jesus, a life of suffering, is just such a tracing tablet. We, the learners of Jesus, have to trace this life, beginning from alpha and going on to omega.

Jesus was homeless; we are pilgrims and sojourners. Here we have no continuing city. Jesus was misunderstood. We also will be misunderstood and mistreated—by Gentiles and even by other Christians. Remember, it was Jesus' own people, the Jews, who rejected him. We should not be surprised if Christians mistreat us. As the Jews were moved by envy and jealousy to dispose of Jesus, Christians have also been known to do the same to other Christians. To be criticized, misunderstood, and rejected causes anguish. But we must remember that other Christians, beginning with the apostles, have gone through far greater trials. Many of them became martyrs for Christ.

Although martyrdom may not be our allotted portion, suffering is. God uses it to conform us to the image of his Son. He uses it to break down our natural man so that we can be reshaped into Christ's image. When the blow comes, our first reaction may be to defy the Potter. We protest with vehement complaints when he attempts to remold us. But when we recognize that it is our Father's hand, we tend to acquiesce with submissive humility. Suffering humbles us; it makes us pliable in the Potter's hand. We must trust that he knows what he is doing. Although we have a difficult time recognizing this while we are passing through the trial, when the ordeal is finished, we realize that it was God working all things together for our good.

We need not pray for sufferings; they will come according to God's design. But we should try to avoid those sufferings that are caused by our own foolishness or sin. There is suffering for foolishness' sake and suffering for righteousness' sake. The former works woe; the latter works in us an exceeding weight of glory. Each time we suffer at the hands of God, the aim is for us to become more and more dependent on him and less and less dependent on self. Look at the life of Jacob, of Joseph, of Daniel, of Peter, and of Paul. All the sufferings they experienced brought them to greater and greater dependence on God. He is doing the same in all of his children. Through it all, we grow to love the Lord more, and we continually come to recognize that nothing can separate us from the love of God in Christ Jesus our Lord. God loves us and is working out the very best for us, all in accord with his desire to have many sons conformed to the image of his unique, beloved Son.

God may have a different, specific design for each of his children, but all of us are on the same pathway to glory. It is natural for us to look at our brothers and sisters, and wonder why we aren't going through what they are or vice versa. Only the Lord knows. He urges us to follow him and live to him; he will take care of the others who are following. Recall how Peter wanted to know how Jesus would lead John (see John 21). After Peter heard from Jesus that his life would end on the cross, Peter asked, "And what about this man [John]?" Jesus told Peter, "If I desire that he remains until I come, what is that to you? You follow me!" (John 21:22). The Lord may take a brother or sister through some trials (or even give him or her some blessings) that we don't understand. We must trust, nevertheless, that he is in God's will. It is the Lord who is leading many sons into glory. Praise him!

A Journey into Glory

The Christian life is a journey—a journey to full sonship, to Christ-likeness, to glory. What a high calling we have! We are not called to a place, but to a Person. One day we will see him, and we shall be like him, for we shall see him as he is (1 John 3:2). Heaven is not our goal; Christ-likeness is. After all, heaven is only a temporary abode for God's believers. In the end, we will dwell on the new earth in the New Jerusalem—a city that comes down out of heaven from God (Rev. 21:10). Yes, we anticipate that city, but participation in that city, we must remember, comes as a benefit of being one of God's sons. The real prize is that we will be with God and he will be with us; we will enjoy him in his Son, the Lamb.

Until that glorious day, we are on a journey—or we might call it a race. Either way, we are here on earth as sojourners and/or runners. Our Pioneer paved the way before us. Through his death on the cross he provides us all with direct access to the Father. We can now come to the Holy of Holies because of Jesus' shed blood and the eternal redemption that blood bought. Through Jesus we have access in one Spirit to the Father (Eph. 2:18). Day by day we endeavor to enter into fellowship with him who is within the veil. This calls for endurance and repeated practice, much like that exercised by a long-distance runner or cross-country hiker. The ultimate goal of the Christian race is to enter permanently into complete and perfect fellowship with the Triune God. At the present, you and I drift in and out of fellowship. Mundane affairs distract us; our mortal bodies confine us. But in that day we will be liberated from our mortality so that we can enjoy unhindered, unlimited fellowship with God.

For this journey God has given us the best provisions. First and foremost, he has given us himself. He has not left us alone. He is not just sitting far away in heaven, waiting to see if we will make it or not. If he were not with us en route, none of us could make it. When Moses was leading the Israelites on their exodus from Egypt to Canaan, he had one preeminent request to bring before God: "if your presence will not go with me, do not carry us up from here" (Exod. 33:15). The most precious provision we have is his presence. Take that away and we have nothing. The Lord's presence should mean everything to us. Nothing is as precious as he himself. It is said that John Wesley on his deathbed repeatedly exclaimed, "The best of all is God is with us!"

Jesus is not far away from us; he is within us! But the Christian life is so paradoxical. On the one hand, we can say that Christ, the all-sufficient One, is in us; on the other hand, we must admit that Christ is in heaven far above us. He is with us and yet not with us. We have Christ via the Spirit of Christ, and yet we look to be with him someday. It is a mystery. What we enjoy of Christ in this life is a foretaste, a sample of what we will enjoy of him in eternity. That is why we are satisfied with Christ today and yet not completely satisfied, for we long for the full taste. Something in our being, though content with him, wants him to return—that we might be with him forever. Until that day, we walk by faith.

For now, Christ is in us by faith; then, we shall see him face to face. We eagerly anticipate that day, the day in which there will be the glorious manifestation of the sons of God. In fact, all of creation awaits the day, for then it will be liberated (together with God's sons) from all the bondage and corruption (see Rom. 8:20–23). In this day, the glory is hidden within us; in that day, it will be completely unveiled. God will be glorified in his children—glorified to the fullest extent, without limitation. He will come to be glorified in his believers and be marveled at in all the believers (2 Thess. 1:10). His glory in the church now is limited due to the limitations of our mortality; in that day, when mortality is completely annihilated, God will be completely magnified in his sons and daughters. In this day, we may appear to be like all those around us; but in that day, the glory will shine through! God will be glorified in his children. This will give him the greatest satisfaction, and his heart's desire will be fulfilled. In that day there will be nothing but praise!

Read the Book of Revelation; see how the believers are enraptured with praise. The Father will be praised as never before, and so will the Son, the Lamb of God. Praise the Father because he is the initiator, the originator of the eternal plan for man. Praise the Father for he is the source, the fountainhead of the divine life that was imparted to us. Praise the Son, the Lamb of God, for he is the one who was willing to carry out the plan of God—to become a man, to die on the cross, to be resurrected, to ascend, and to send his Spirit to indwell the believers. The Lamb is worthy of all our praise! All of the believers in that day, great and small, will have equal status before the Lamb; all will be equally humbled before and enthralled with the glorious Lamb! All differences will have faded in his presence. You and I, together with the heroes of faith, will all fall before the Lamb and shout, "Hallelujah to the Lamb!" and "Lamb of God, you are worthy!"

This will not be a totally new experience as much as it will be a totally full experience. In this day we have been given the foretaste of that coming glory. I cannot count the number of times that I, together with the believers assembled around the Lord's table, have enjoyed praising the Father and the Lamb in a way that undeniably previewed the day of glory. The presence of the Triune God was so unmistakably real. Our older brother Jesus was in our midst leading the hymns of praise to the Father and bringing us into his presence of absolute stillness and perfect peace. In his presence there is nothing to say, nothing to do. It is perfect contentment, like that of a child resting on the Father's bosom. That experience is worth all the trials and sufferings of the Christian life.

Unfortunately, that sweet contentment in the Father's presence is evanescent. Almost as soon as we settle down in his arms, we become unsettled again. The hymn ends, the praises cease, the meeting is over. We go home to face, once again, the life we must all endure. The memory of that experience give us hope and encouragement to press on. One day the meeting won't end and the hymns won't cease; one day we will never again leave the glorious, sweet loving presence of our Father. We will be with him and he with us forever; we will see his face and he will wipe away all the tears from our eyes.

Notes

Introduction

[1]Aune, *New Testament in Its Literary Environment,* 18.
[2]Ryken, *Literature of the Bible,* 273.
[3]Aune, *New Testament in Its Literary Environment,* 29.
[4]Ibid., 34.
[5]Robinson, *Priority of John,* 92.
[6]Aune, *New Testament in Its Literary Environment,* 63–64.
[7]Ibid., 66–67.
[8]Ibid., 122–24; Scholes and Kellogg, *Nature of Narrative,* 73–79.
[9]Segovia, "Journeys of the Word of God," 33–34.
[10]Ibid., 47.
[11]Moberly, *Atonement and Personality,* 168.
[12]Culpepper, *Johannine School,* 261–90.
[13]Culpepper, *Anatomy of the Fourth Gospel,* 206–23.
[14]Dodd, *Interpretation of the Fourth Gospel,* 316–17.
[15]Culpepper, *Anatomy of the Fourth Gospel,* 226.
[16]Brown, *Gospel According to John I–XII,* lxxviii.

Chapter 1: Prologue to the Journey

[1]Schnakenburg makes much of this—with some good insights, but his exegesis of the prologue contains too much conjecture about John's use of a particular "Logos Hymn," while such a hymn is not extant.

[2]See Beasley-Murray for a full discussion on the poetic structure of the prologue.

[3]The first clause of the prologue could be translated "In eternity the Word existed" or "As to a beginning, the Word already was." Or it is possible that the first line is an incipit title, that is, the title is inherent in the beginning line, as in Mark 1:1. If so, John 1:1 could be translated "In beginning [this story]: There was the Word, and the Word was with God, and the Word was God."

[4]In defense of this view is the fact that John 1:2 clearly presents the Word's eternality. If John had meant to affirm the Word's eternality in the first verse, the second would be but a hollow repetition. Thus, it is possible that John was simply starting the book with a description of Jesus Christ who was the Word, who was with God, and who was God. Then, in the second verse, John affirmed that he was with God from the very beginning—and in the third that he worked with God in creating the universe. Verses 4 and 5, then, relate something about Jesus' mission on earth as the light of life.

[5]In the expression "the Word was with God," there is an article before God *(ton theon)*, pointing to God the Father. In the expression "the Word was God," there is no article before "God." The distinction may indicate that John did not want the reader to think that the Son was the Father, but was the same as the Father; that is, both are God, both are *theos.*

[6]See Williams' translation, *The New Testament in the Language of the People.* The preposition "with" in Greek is *pros,* associated with the Greek expression *prosōpon pros prosōpon,* meaning "face to face with." The expression was commonly used in Greek language to indicate a personal relationship.

[7]The New Testament reveals that the Son of God was the agent of creation, for all things were created through him (see 1 Cor. 8:6; Col. 1:16; Heb. 1:2).

[8]Because 1:4 follows a verse pertaining to the Word's role in creation, some commentators think that 1:4 belongs to the period prior to Christ's incarnation. This view is especially favored by those who prefer to punctuate 1:3–4 the way it appears in UBS[4] and NA[26]. They see the preincarnate Word, as God, giving life and light to men (see Ps. 36:9). Although this interpretation is possible, it must be remembered that John did not maintain a strict chronology throughout his prologue. For example, 1:9–12 clearly identifies the time of Christ's incarnation and yet it is not until 1:14 that John says that "the Word became flesh." Furthermore, it should be said that 1:1–5 forms a kind of miniprologue to and within the whole prologue (1:1–18). Thus, it is more likely that 1:4 pertains to the ministry of Jesus Christ begun in the flesh and now continued in the Spirit—for the light continues to shine. The present tense verb shows that John was thinking of the effect of Christ's life and message even after his ministry on earth (see 1 John 2:8, which says "the darkness is passing away, and the true light is now shining").

[9]The expression *erchomenon eis ton kosmon* (coming into the world) is ambiguous. According to the Greek grammar, this phrase can modify *to phōs* (the light) or *panta anthrōpon* (every person). According to the general drift of the prologue, John was speaking about the light coming into the world. But it is possible that John was speaking of every person's entrance into the world. As such, the prologue alludes to the intersection of Jesus' entrée into the world with that of everyone else's. Everyone has had a chance to respond to the light.

[10]Many modern translators have rendered this phrase "the Word became a man." Of course, this is what the text means. But John purposely used the word "flesh" because he was either (1) combatting a heresy called Docetism (a heresy that denied the actuality of Jesus Christ's human body) or (2) emphasizing the physical limitations of Jesus' human existence. The Docetists claimed that the Son of God merely assumed the guise of humanity but did not actually partake of it. In his first epistle, John said that any person who did not confess that Jesus Christ had come in flesh was a person who did not belong to God (1 John 4:3). It was important for John to show that God fully participated in the human experience.

[11]According to the best manuscripts, the text reads *monogenēs theos,* which means "an only One, God" or "God, the only begotten." This is supported by P66 Aleph* B C* L. A few other manuscripts (P75 Aleph[1] 33) read *ho monogenēs theos* (the only begotten God). All other manuscripts, most of which are quite late, read *ho monogenēs huios* (the only begotten Son). The manuscript evidence for the first reading (basically supported by the second reading) is superior to the evidence for the third reading. The papyri (P66 and P75—which adds the article *ho*), the earliest uncials (Aleph B C), and some early versions (Coptic and Syriac) support the first reading.

[12]Or, "he has narrated him." This translation, as the one above, supplies a direct object. Without an object, it could be rendered, "he has made his explanation"—that is, the Word's life on earth provided a full explanation of God to men. We derive the English word "exegesis" from the Greek verb *exēgeomai,* meaning, "to lead through," "to narrate," or "to draw out."

Chapter 2: Being the First Followers in the Journey

[1]The Greek word for "takes away" *(airō)* can also mean "take up" or "bear." Jesus took away our sin by taking it upon himself and bearing it. This is the image conveyed in Isa. 53 (see also 1 Pet. 2:24). Note that the text says "sin" and not "sins"; Jesus would take away the sin principle that had plagued the world since the fall of Adam (Rom. 5:12–21).

[2]Even though the alternative reading, "the Son of God," has good external support (P66 P75 A B C W), it is more likely that the reading "the chosen One of God" (found in P5[vid] Aleph) was changed to "the Son of God" than vice versa. For example, Gordon Fee thinks an orthodox scribe of the second century might have sensed "the possibility that the designation 'Chosen One' might be used to support adoptionism and so altered the text for orthodox reasons" (see Fee's article, "The Textual Criticism of the New Testament," in *The Expositor's Bible Commentary,* 1:431–32). Furthermore, it has been urged by James Williams in an article, "Renderings from Some Johannine Passages" (*The Bible Translator* 25, no. 3 [July 1974]: 352–53) that the title "chosen One" adds one more messianic title to the chain of witnesses in John 1, while "Son" is repetitive (see 1:14, 49).

[3]Philip and Bartholomew are paired together in the list of the disciples in Matt. 10:3 and Mark 3:18; here Nathanael and Philip are paired up.

[4]The Messiah was to be born in Bethlehem (Mic. 5:2); and, in fact, Jesus was born in Bethlehem. But his parents' flight to Egypt and later return to Galilee, where Jesus was reared, gave him the reputation of being a Galilean, specifically a Nazarene from the hill country of Nazareth. This was a cause of stumbling for many Jews, because they could not accept a Messiah who had not come from Bethlehem. And since Jesus never told them this, they continued to believe that he was reared from birth as a Galilean, as a Nazarene.

[5]The Greek word for "guile" *(dolos)* was originally used to designate a trap. Taken figuratively, the word means "deceit, cunning, falsehood."

[6]Some commentators think Nathanael's revelation is too full and too sudden; thus, they say these words must have been put on his lips by the author for dramatic effect. But Nathanael was a seeker whose heart was pure, and Jesus promised that the pure in heart would see God (Matt. 5:8).

[7]This outburst from Nathanael is so reflective of Psalm 2 that one wonders if that is the passage he was reading under the fig tree.

[8]This is the first time in this Gospel that Jesus calls himself "the Son of Man." This title was his favorite self-designation; he applied it to himself to identify with the messianic title contained in Dan. 7:14 and to present himself as a man among men—living in full identification with humanity, as the God who became man, the God-man. The entire first chapter of John attributes the highest titles to Jesus. He is called the Word, God, the one and only Son, the Christ, the King of Israel; but Jesus, when speaking of himself, preferred to call himself "the Son of Man."

[9]MacGregor, *Gospel of John,* 52.

Chapter 3: Revealing the New Temple and Kingdom

[1]The Greek word *naos* refers to the inner sanctuary (i.e., the Holy Place and the Holy of Holies). Another Greek word is also translated "temple" in John 2:14–15; the word is *hieron.* It refers to the temple proper, including the outer courts. When Jesus cleansed the temple, he only cleansed a portion of the outer courts. When Jesus spoke of the temple that would be destroyed, he was speaking of his body as the inner sanctuary, the place of God's dwelling.

[2]According to the Greek, Jesus said, "*You* destroy this temple." (The verb is second person plural aorist active imperative.) He did not say he would destroy the temple. But at the time of Jesus' trial, some of his accusers twisted his statement to assert that Jesus said

he would destroy the temple (Matt. 26:61; Mark 14:58). This was the only accusation against Jesus that was clearly verbalized, and the accusation was false.

[3]In 2:23–24, John used the Greek verb *pisteuō* (to trust) to make a word play, as is conveyed in the following rendering: "many *trusted* in his name . . . but he did not *entrust* himself to them."

[4]This interpretation is based on the verbal connection between 2:25 ("Jesus knew what was in man") and 3:1 ("there was a man . . . named Nicodemus").

[5]This is the reading in the earliest manuscripts; other manuscripts read, "God gives him [Jesus] the Spirit without limit." The statement could mean that God gives the immeasurable Spirit—in this case, to his Son, or that Jesus gives the immeasurable Spirit—when he speaks the words of God. It can be argued that Jesus Christ dispensed the Spirit via his spoken word, since John 6:63 says that his words are spirit. But many commentators favor the second option, primarily because the next verse speaks of the Father giving all things to the Son. As such, the Son was the recipient of the immeasurable Spirit for his prophetic ministry (see Isa. 11:1–2).

Chapter 4: Following the Savior of the World

[1]John, the writer, spoke of the well as a fountain *(pēgē)* in verse 6, and Jesus described the gift of God as a fountain *(pēgē)* in verse 14.

[2]The expression, "gathers fruit into eternal life," draws upon the image of grain being brought into the barn at harvest time (Matt. 13:30; Luke 3:17). The "fruit" are those who believe in Jesus as the Christ, and as a result of their faith, are given eternal life.

[3]Admittedly, there are problems with this interpretation. First, John 4:1–3 may indicate that Jesus left Judea, not because he was rejected, but because his popularity was growing there. Second, in all the other Gospels Jesus' statement about not being received in his own country is spoken with respect to being rejected in his own hometown, Nazareth of Galilee. In all three occurrences (Matt. 13:57; Mark 6:4; Luke 4:24), the word *patridi* is used to describe Nazareth. Therefore, it is questionable that Jesus thought of Judea as his *patridi* ("native country"). Finally, it could be argued that the passage that follows (vv. 46–54) is ironic—it speaks of apparent reception but actual rejection. In other words, the Galileans welcomed him as a miracle-worker but not as a prophet, much less the Messiah (see v. 48). Nevertheless, the most satisfying solution to this exegetical dilemma is to reckon "Judea" as the native country from which Jesus was rejected.

[4]The most obvious difference between John 4:46–54 and Matt. 8:5–13 and Luke 7:1–10 is that John speaks of the healing of the official's son, while Matthew and Luke speak of the centurion's servant. However, Matthew's terminology, *pais*, need not be restricted to "slave"; it can also mean "child." If so, only Luke (who uses *doulos*) speaks of the healed person as a slave. This would bind Matthew and John together in a closer unity, both lexically and spiritually, in that Matthew's account emphasizes Jesus' inclusion of a Gentile in the kingdom.

Chapter 5: Hearing the Life-Giver and Judge

[1]According to most manuscripts (P66 P75 A B D W^s), there is no article before "festival." Thus, the festival is unspecified. Only two manuscripts (Aleph C) read "the festival of the Jews." Undoubtedly, the scribes of these manuscripts (and other later ones) added the definite article before "festival" in an attempt to designate a specific feast (as either Passover, Pentecost, or Tabernacles). Many early Greek fathers (such as John Chrysostom and Cyril of Alexandria) believed it was Pentecost, which would help explain the references to Moses in the discourse (5:46–47), "for in that process which connected originally agricultural feasts to events in Israel's history, the Feast of Weeks (Pentecost) was identified with the

celebration of Moses' receiving the Law on Mount Sinai" (Brown, *Gospel According to John I–XII*, 206). Perhaps the scribes of Aleph and C also believed it was the Festival of Pentecost and therefore added a definite article.

[2]The signs in John's Gospel became progressively greater: water changed to wine (chap. 2), healing of a sick boy (chap. 4), healing of an invalid (chap. 5), feeding the five thousand (chap. 6), giving sight to a blind man (chap. 9), and raising Lazarus from the dead (chap. 11).

[3]When Jesus said, "A time is coming and has now come when the dead will hear the voice of the Son of God and those who hear will live," he perceived the eschatological moment as happening in the present. Reception of eternal life is a present experience assuring eternal life in the future. In the future, the physically dead will hear the Son of God's voice and will be raised from the grave (see 5:28).

[4]In saying this about John the Baptist, Jesus was showing that John's witness fulfilled messianic prophecy: "I will cause the horn of David to spring forth; I have prepared a lamp for my anointed One" (Ps. 132:17).

[5]There is no verse in the Old Testament that explicitly states that eternal life can be obtained by studying the Scriptures. However, some rabbis must have thought so. Hillel said, "The more study of the law the more life, . . . if one has gained for himself words of the law he has gained for himself life in the age to come" (*Pirqe 'Aboth* 2.7).

Chapter 6: Giving Manna from Heaven

[1]Many commentators see a connection between the Passover (mentioned in 6:4) and Jesus offering himself as the bread of life because the Passover symbolizes God's provision for life and salvation (see 1 Cor. 5:7).

[2]The first sentence can be translated two ways: (1) "It was not Moses who has given you the bread from heaven" or (2) "Moses has not given you the bread from heaven." The first negates Moses as the giver; the second negates the action of giving. In either case, the tense is perfect, thereby emphasizing the fact that Moses—then or now—had not given them any kind of lasting bread. Then, Jesus shifted to the present tense: "It is my Father who gives you the true bread from heaven." The Father who continually gave the manna to the Israelites is the One who gives (and keeps on giving) the true bread out of heaven. Again, the idea of the continual supply is emphasized by the present tense: "For the bread of God is he who comes down from heaven and gives life to the world." Just as manna came down every day, so the Son, as it were, comes down continually (not in the sense of repeated incarnations but in the sense of an abiding presence) and keeps on giving life to the world (not just to the Jews).

[3]Jesus had moved from Nazareth to Capernaum at the beginning of his ministry (see Matt. 4:13; Mark 1:21; John 2:12); most likely, his parents and siblings went with him. The Jews in Capernaum knew Jesus' parents and therefore they thought they knew who Jesus was—the son of Joseph.

[4]The words *pan ho* (all that) in the Greek text of 6:37 and 6:39 are neuter singular; they indicate the total collective entity of all believers, which is given as a gift to the Son from the Father. These verses also speak about individual believers. They can be assured that once they come to Jesus they will not be cast out (cf. 10:28–29).

[5]At this time in Jesus' ministry there were several following him who could loosely be called "his disciples" (see 4:1).

[6]The reading "the Holy One of God" is superior to all the other readings because of its excellent documentary support (P75 Aleph B C* D L W) and because most of the other variant readings are obvious scribal assimilations to Matt. 16:16 ("the Christ, the Son of the living God") or some derivation thereof.

Chapter 7: Journeying with the Smitten Rock and Light of Life

[1]Most likely, the Jews were amazed that Jesus could interpret the Scriptures the way in which the rabbis did without having the same education they received. The same amazement is expressed in Matt. 7:28–29 (and cf. Acts 4:13, where the disciples are called "unlettered men").

[2]There is no single verse in the Old Testament that exactly says "out of his innermost being [lit. belly] will flow rivers of living water." Jesus was either paraphrasing a verse like Ps. 78:16 ("He brought forth streams also from the rock, and caused waters to run down like rivers"), or a verse like Isa. 58:11 ("you will be like a watered garden, and like a spring of water whose waters do not fail"). The psalm passage is the nearest to what Jesus said and affirms that Jesus was speaking about himself as the antitype of the smitten rock.

[3]Various scribes could not resist the temptation to add the word "Holy" as a descriptor to "the Spirit," an addition that frequently happened throughout the course of the transmission of the New Testament text, and/or to add "given." Most translators (except those of the NJB and NRSV) have also felt compelled to add the word "given." But this addition slightly modifies the meaning of the original wording.

[4]John 7:53–8:11 was not part of John's original composition. This passage, known as the pericope about the adulteress, is not included in any of the earliest manuscripts (P66 P75 Aleph A^vid B C^vid L T W and several ancient versions). Its first appearance in a Greek manuscript is in D, but it is not contained in other Greek manuscripts until the ninth century. When this story is inserted in later manuscripts, it appears in different places (after John 7:52, after Luke 21:38, at the end of John) and when it does appear it is often marked off by asterisks or obeli to signal its probable spuriousness. The story may have been part of an oral tradition that was included in the Syriac Peshitta, circulated in the Western church, eventually finding its way into the Latin Vulgate, and from there into later Greek manuscripts, the like of which were used in formulating the Textus Receptus.

The internal evidence against Johannine authorship is also impressive. First of all, many scholars have pointed out that the vocabulary used in this pericope does not accord with the rest of John. Second, the insertion of the pericope adulteress at this point in John (after 7:52 and before 8:12) greatly disrupts the narrative flow. Westcott and Hort indicated that the setting of John 7 and 8 is at Jerusalem during the Festival of Tabernacles. During this festival, the Jews would customarily pour water over a rock (in commemoration of the water supply coming from the smitten rock in the wilderness) and light lamps (in commemoration of the pillar of light that accompanied the Israelites in their wilderness journey). With reference to these two ritualistic enactments, Jesus presented himself as the true source of living water (John 7:37–39) and as the true light to be followed (John 8:12). Westcott and Hort's argument is that the pericope about the adulteress disrupts the continuity between the events (*Notes*, 87–88). For a more detailed discussion on this, see my article, "The Pericope of the Adulteress" in *The Bible Translator*, Jan. 1989.

Chapter 8: Presenting the I AM

[1]John 8:12 was included in the previous chapter because it presents Jesus as fulfilling the two key aspects of the Festival of Tabernacles: the water of life and the light of life. It was also included in the previous chapter because this verse (excluding the pericope of the adulteress) is thematically linked with 7:52. But John 8:12 also belongs with this chapter because it contains the first of an eightfold series of "I am" declarations in John 8.

[2]There are three ways to translate Jesus' response in this verse: (1) "[I am] principally that which I also speak to you"; (2) "[I am] what I have been telling you from the beginning"; (3) "Why do I speak to you at all?" The first and second translations are based on a text that reads *tēn archēn ho ti kai lalō humin*; the third, on the reading *tēn archēn hoti kai lalō humin*.

Because so many early Greek manuscripts did not leave any spaces between words, it is difficult to determine if the text should read *ho ti* (that which) or *hoti* (why). Two early manuscripts, P75 and B, have a space between *ho* and *ti;* another early manuscript, P66, does not. The corrector of P66 added *eipon humin* (I said) before the phrase noted above. This gives the rendering: "I told you in the beginning that which I also speak to you." Only a few scholars favor this reading.

[3]The Jews were offended to hear anything about needing liberation, for they were convinced that they, as Abraham's descendants, had never been slaves of anyone. Hadn't their ancestors been enslaved to the Egyptians, to the Assyrians, and to the Babylonians? And weren't they under the yoke of Roman rule at the moment Jesus spoke? And were they not looking to the Messiah to free them from Roman domination? But Jesus was speaking of the liberation of the soul set free from sin. He would have to die to give them this freedom.

[4]The reading in P66 Aleph[c] A B[c] C D L is "and you have seen Abraham?" A few other early manuscripts (P75 Aleph*) read, "and Abraham has seen you?" The second reading, though fairly well supported, appears to be an assimilation to the preceding verse in which Jesus indicated that Abraham rejoiced to see his day. The first reading, being more difficult and having better external attestation, is perhaps the correct one. Jesus had not claimed to be a contemporary with Abraham or that he had seen Abraham; he had said that Abraham had seen his day.

Chapter 9: Leading God's People from Darkness to Light

[1]This is the reading in NA[26]/UBS[4], supported by Aleph[c] A B C D 0124. But according to early and good manuscript support (P66 P75 Aleph* L W), the last pronoun is *hēmas* (us): "we must work the works of him who sent us." This reading explicitly includes the disciples as "sent ones."

[2]In 9:38 and the first part of 9:39 ("And he said, 'I believe, Lord'; and he worshiped him. And Jesus said") are not included in P75, Aleph*, W, Coptic manuscripts, and the Diatessaron. It could be argued that the omission may be the result of a transcriptional error, but not in so many diverse manuscripts. Brown suggests that the words may be "an addition stemming from the association of John ix with the baptismal liturgy and catechesis" (*Gospel According to John I–XII*, 375). Calvin Porter makes a strong argument for this portion being a liturgical addition. See his article, "John IX. 38, 39a: A Liturgical Addition to the Text," *New Testament Studies* 13 (1967): 387–94.

[3]The Greek expression *aposunagōgos genetai* literally means "become de-synagogued"— similar to the idea of excommunication. The expression is uniquely Johannine (used here and in 12:42; 16:2).

[4]All the earliest manuscripts (P66 P75 Aleph B D W) read "the Son of Man." Later manuscripts read "the Son of God." It is far more likely that "man" *(anthrōpou)* was changed to "God" *(theou)* than vice versa. The title "the Son of Man" was a surrogate for "Messiah." Later in history, the church sought confession of Jesus' divine sonship—hence, the change from "the Son of Man" to "the Son of God" in later manuscripts.

[5]Jesus himself was even considered a *lēstēs* by the authorities who arrested him (Matt. 26:55). This may shed new light on why Jesus was crucified with two "thieves."

Chapter 10: Consecrating a New Habitation for God

[1]The festival, called Hanukkah, is held in December and lasts eight days. Similar to the Feast of Tabernacles, it was a time of great rejoicing. (For the history of this event see 1 Macc. 4:36–59; 2 Macc. 1:9; 10:1–8). Bruce wrote, "To this day it is celebrated as the Feast of lights, so called from the lighting of the lamps or candles in Jewish homes to honor the occasion" (*Gospel of John,* 230).

[2]Brown, *Gospel According to John I–XII*, 402.

[3]By contrast, it was safe for Jesus to tell a Samaritan woman he was the Messiah (John 4:25–26).

[4]Two variant readings in this verse support this view: (1) "that which my Father has given me is greater than all" in B*, and (2) "my Father, as to that which he has given me, is greater than all" in Aleph D L W. Elsewhere in his Gospel, John used the neuter singular to designate the corporate entity of believers (which encompasses all Christians as one unit) that was given to him as a gift from the Father (see 6:37, 39; 17:2, 24). Given the context of John 10, Jesus would be saying that this one corporate entity (which could be called the church), which was given to the Son by the Father and was under the protective care of the Father's hand and the Son's hand, would be invincible to the attack of the enemy (see vv. 1, 5, 8, 10, 12) and therefore would be greater than all (i.e., greater than all the enemies mentioned in John 10).

Other manuscripts read, "My Father, who has given them to me, is greater than all." This is found in P66ᶜ and P75ᵛⁱᵈ. This reading also makes good sense and has early support.

[5]According to excellent documentary support (P45 P66 P75 B L W), the verse contains the Greek word *ginōskō* twice, in two tenses (aorist and present), suggesting inceptive knowledge and continuous knowledge.

Chapter 11: Raising the Dead

[1]Adapted from Comfort and Hawley, *Opening the Gospel of John*, 179.

Life that is really life (1 Tim. 6:19) is by its very nature resurrection life, because it can stand the trial of death. Only one kind of life—the life of God (Eph. 4:18), the indissoluble life (Heb. 7:16), designated *zōē* in the New Testament—is truly life.

[2]Note the perfect tense in 11:27: "I have believed." This denotes that her past belief is still very much present.

[3]Many modern translators have tried to soften the text by saying Jesus was "deeply moved" (see NIV, TEV, NEB). This was done by ancient scribes as well. The original hand of P66 reads, "he was agitated in his spirit and troubled in himself." This was corrected to read, "he was troubled in his spirit as if agitated." This is also the reading in P45ᵛⁱᵈ D and some other witnesses. The correction displays a scribal attempt to soften the statement about Jesus' agitation and anger.

Chapter 12: Coming into His Glory

[1]According to the NRSV, the text reads, "Leave her alone. She bought it so that she might keep it for the day of my burial. You always have the poor with you, but you do not always have me." Something needs to be supplied before the *hina* clause. The NRSV adds "she bought it" and the NIV adds "it was intended." Another way to translate this sentence is, "You should have let her keep this for the day of my burial."

[2]The last part of 12:6 can be translated "he carried the money bag" or "he took [lit. lifted] what was in the money bag." The context favors the second rendering, which is quite close to our modern idiom, "shoplifting."

[3]John 12:23–24 reads: "The hour has come for the Son of Man to be glorified. Truly, truly, I say unto you, unless a grain of wheat falls into the ground and dies, it abides alone; but if it dies, it brings forth many grains." Jesus' declaration provides the best picture of resurrection. Paul also used this illustration. He likened the resurrection glory to a grain being sown in death, then coming forth in life (see 1 Cor. 15:35–45).

[4]The text reads: "And I, if [when] I am lifted up from the earth, will draw all men to myself. But this he said to show what kind of death he was about to die." As earlier (see 3:14; 8:28),

Jesus again speaks of his death in terms of "being lifted up." John's following explanation makes it clear that this expression signified the mode of execution—the cross, upon which the executed was lifted up. But there is a double significance to the expression "lifted up": it means lifted up on the cross and lifted up in exaltation. Actually, Jesus' death on the cross was the first stage of his exaltation. In his exalted state, Jesus, the crucified one, draws the believers to himself.

Chapter 13: Serving the Believers

[1]If this meal was the Passover meal, then any subsequent verses in John that mention a feast yet to come must refer to the Feast of Unleavened Bread, not to the Passover meal (13:29; 18:28; 19:14). In New Testament times the Passover and the Feast of Unleavened Bread were used interchangeably.

[2]"Judas" is nominative in the earliest and best manuscripts (P66 Aleph B W L 0124), and genitive ("of Judas") in later and inferior manuscripts (A D Maj).

[3]If the phrase "except for his feet" belongs to the original text (as in P66 B and C), then Jesus was speaking of two kinds of bathing—the first, a bath of the whole body, and the second, a washing of the feet. If the Gospel originally did not include the phrase "except the feet" (as in Aleph and Origen), then Jesus was telling Peter that the initial bath was sufficient; there was no further need for cleansing.

[4]The expression "to lift up the heel" in Hebrew means "he has made his heel great against me"—that is, "has given me a great fall" or "has taken cruel advantage of me" (Bruce).

Chapter 14: Preparing the Way to the Father

[1]Some manuscripts (Aleph[2] A C[2] Maj) begin the verse with the phrase "if God is [lit. was] glorified in him," but the phrase is not present in the earliest witnesses (P66 Aleph* B C*) and in other manuscripts (D L W). Many scholars think the phrase is an intrinsic part of John's original writing, and that it was omitted from many manuscripts because of homoeoteleuton or deliberate deletion of perceived redundancy (see 13:31).

[2]Westcott, *The Gospel According to St. John,* 196.

[3]Robert Gundry, "In My Father's House Are Many Monai," *Zeitschrift für neutestamentliche Wissenschaft* 58 (1967): 68–72.

[4]One text (supported by P66 Aleph D W) reads, "if you have known me, you will know my Father also"; another text (supported by A B C L Maj) reads, "if you had known me, you would have known my Father also." The textual evidence is divided. Internal considerations favor the second reading because it seems more likely that Jesus was reproving the disciples than promising them.

[5]Morris, *Gospel According to John,* 651.

Chapter 15: Planting a New Vine

[1]Pink, *Exposition of the Gospel of John,* 400.

[2]Morris, *Gospel According to John,* 670.

[3]Robertson, *Word Pictures in the Greek New Testament,* 5:258–59.

[4]Murray, *True Vine,* 50.

[5]Three words are used quite frequently in Jesus' last discourse: "command," "commands," and "words." The commands are summed up in one command: "love one another" (see John 13:34; 15:17; 1 John 3:23–24), and the Lord's words are the specific utterances (Greek *rhēmata*) he gives to us.

Chapter 16: Sending the Spirit of Reality

[1]It is appropriate to include John 14:26 here because it was not discussed in detail in Chapter 14, and because it has a close exegetical relationship with 15:26 and 16:1–13.

[2]Morris, *Gospel According to John,* 697–99.

[3]Ibid., 699.

[4]Olshausen cited by Alford, *Greek New Testament,* 1:870.

Chapter 17: Praying for Oneness

[1]Paul used a Greek word in Ephesians 1:5, 9, 11 that conveys the idea of desire, even heart's desire. The word is usually translated as "will"—"the will of God." But the English word "will" sublimates the primary meaning. The Greek word *(thelēma)* is primarily an emotional word and secondarily volitional. "God's will" is not so much "God's intention" as it is "God's heart's desire." God does have an intention, a purpose, a plan. It is called *prothesis* in Greek (see Eph. 1:11) and it literally means "a laying out beforehand" (like a blueprint). This plan was created by God's counsel (called *boulē* in Greek, Eph. 1:11). But behind the plan and the counsel was not just a mastermind but a heart of love and of good pleasure. Therefore, Paul talks about "the good pleasure of God's heart's desire" (1:5). Paul also says, "he made known to us the mystery of his heart's desire, according to his good pleasure which he purposed in him" (1:9). Indeed, God operates all things according to the counsel of his heart's desire (1:11).

[2]The word "sonship" is inclusive; it incorporates both male and female believers.

[3]I use the term "sons" because it is the term found in the Scriptures—with one exception in the New Testament, 2 Corinthians 6:18, in which God's people are called "sons and daughters."

[4]In both 17:11 and 17:12 the best manuscripts (P66[vid] Aleph B C W) read, "keep them in the name that you have given me." Other manuscripts (such as D, some later miniscules, and some early versions) read "keep in your name those whom you have given me." The original text indicates that Jesus had been given the Father's name.

[5]Excellent manuscript evidence (P60 Aleph B D W) supports the reading "that which you have given me," as opposed to the reading found in some manuscripts (A C L), "those whom you have given me."

Chapter 18: Facing Trial

[1]John does not give us any record of the interview Caiaphas must have had with Jesus. The reader is simply told in 18:28 that he was taken from Caiaphas' house to the Praetorium, where he was interrogated by Pilate. By taking into account the record of the Synoptic Gospels, we can assume that the interview with Caiaphas was the same as that in which Jesus appeared before the Sanhedrin—for Caiaphas would have been presiding over the Sanhedrin.

[2]This is a paraphrase.

[3]This idea is captured in the NEB: "Then at last, to satisfy them [the chief priests], he handed over Jesus to be crucified." (The same idea is expressed in Luke 23:35—"he delivered Jesus to their will.")

Chapter 19: Dying on the Cross

[1]This word frequently appears in the nonliterary papyri with this meaning.

[2]The expression "that one knows that he tells the truth" (19:35) has been interpreted in a variety of ways: (a) That one (Christ) knows that he (John, the writer) tells the truth.

Those who support this view say that *ekeinos* is used for "Christ" in 3:28, 30; 7:11; 9:28. (b) That one (God) knows that he (John, the writer) tells the truth. (c) That one (John) knows that he (the writer) tells the truth. In order to accept this interpretation, one must believe that this verse was not written by John but by someone else who published the Gospel in its final edited form. He is herein affirming that the eyewitness (John) knows that he (the writer) is telling the truth. (d) That one (John) knows that he (John) tells the truth. In this case, "that one" is the same as "he who tells the truth." In other words, he used *ekeinos* to speak of himself. The one who saw the crucifixion and witnessed the issue of blood and water was John the apostle. Whatever the interpretation, the intent of the verse is to affirm the veracity of the eyewitness account.

[3]This wording does not appear in every English translation of the New Testament (e.g., RSV, NEB, TEV, JB) because certain translators understood the phrase "from the foundation of the world" to modify "the names not written in the book of life." This syntactical rearrangement is permissible but the order in the Greek has the prepositional phrase "from the foundation of the world" immediately following "the Lamb" (see ASV, NIV, NASB mg, TLB mg.).

Chapter 20: Rising from the Dead

[1]For example, see Bengel's *New Testament Word Studies* and Vincent's *Word Studies in the New Testament* on John 20:22.

[2]See J. B. Phillips' *The New Testament in Modern English*, note on John 20:22.

[3]This is a term used in *The Emphasized Bible* by J. B. Rotherham.

[4]Alford, *Greek Testament*, 4:365.

[5]Milligan, *Resurrection of Our Lord*, 246.

[6]Ibid., 248–56.

[7]Alford, *Greek Testament*, 4:171.

[8]Gaffin, *Centrality of the Resurrection*, 87.

Chapter 21: The Conclusion and Epilogue to the Journey

[1]See Comfort, *Quest for the Original Text of the New Testament*, appendix.

[2]The earliest manuscripts (P66[vid] Aleph* B) read *pisteuēte* (continue to believe), while later manuscripts (Aleph[2] A C D W) read *pisteusēte* (believe). The editors of UBS[4] and NA[26] adopted the second reading, but signaled their doubt about the aorist verb by bracketing the sigma. In this verse John was certifying the trustworthiness of his testimony so that the readers (who were probably already believers) would continue to believe the veracity of the gospel.

[3]I am quite aware of the current trend in Johannine studies that claims that John used many synonyms throughout his Gospel without intending to make any semantic distinctions; but I am not convinced that John, in all instances in which he used synonyms, was simply groping for lexical variation and not semantic difference. John 21:15–17 seems to warrant an exegesis that accounts for a semantic difference between *agapao* and *phileō*.

[4]Bruce, *Gospel of John*, 408.

[5]This truth is elaborated in the next chapter.

[6]Westcott, *Gospel According to St. John*, 306.

Postscript: Thoughts for Our Spiritual Journey

[1]Most translators render the clause "leading many sons into glory" as "bringing many sons to glory" because they place this expression in connection with God the Father. However, the grammar in the original Greek indicates that it is the leader (*archēgon*—

accusative) who does the leading (*agagonta*—also accusative). This was pointed out by Marshall in his introduction to the *Greek-English Interlinear New Testament* (Nestle/Marshall). As such, Hebrews 2:10 could be rendered as follows: "For it is fitting for him, for whom are all things and by whom are all things, to perfect through sufferings the Leader who leads many sons into glory, even the Leader of their salvation."

[2]The Greek word for predestinate, *proorizō,* literally means "to mark out one's destiny beforehand." Our English word "horizon" is a derivative.

References

Aland, Black, Martini, Metzger, Wikgren, eds. *The Greek New Testament.* 4th corrected ed. New York: United Bible Societies, 1993. (Abbreviated as UBS[4])

Alford, Henry. *The Greek Testament.* 1852. Reprint, Grand Rapids: Guardian Press, 1976.

Barrett, C. K. *The Gospel According to St. John.* Philadelphia: Westminster Press, 1978.

Beasley-Murray, George R. *John* in the *Word Biblical Commentary.* Waco, Tex.: Word, 1987.

Bengel, John Albert. *New Testament Word Studies.* 1742. Translated by C. Lewis and M. Vincent. Grand Rapids: Eerdmans, 1971.

Brown, Raymond E. *The Gospel According to John I–XII, XIII–XXI.* New York: Doubleday, 1966, 1970.

Bruce, F. F. *The Gospel of John.* Grand Rapids: Eerdmans, 1983.

Carson, D. A. *The Gospel According to John.* Grand Rapids: Eerdmans, 1989.

Comfort, Philip W. *Early Manuscripts and Modern Translations of the New Testament.* Wheaton: Tyndale House, 1990.

———. *The Quest for the Original Text of the New Testament.* Grand Rapids: Baker, 1992.

Comfort, Philip, and Wendell Hawley. *Opening the Gospel of John.* Wheaton: Tyndale House, 1994.

Culpepper, R. Allen. *The Johannine School.* Missoula, Mont.: Scholars Press, 1975.

———. *Anatomy of the Fourth Gospel: A Study in Literary Design.* Philadelphia: Fortress Press, 1983.

Dodd, C. H. *The Interpretation of the Fourth Gospel.* Cambridge: Cambridge University Press, 1953.

Gaffin, Richard. *The Centrality of the Resurrection.* Grand Rapids: Baker, 1978.

Iser, Wolfgang. *The Implied Reader.* Baltimore: Johns Hopkins University Press, 1974.

MacGregor, G. H. C. *The Gospel of John.* London: Hodder and Stoughton, 1928.

Metzger, Bruce. *A Textual Commentary on the Greek New Testament.* New York: United Bible Societies, 1971.

Milligan, William. *The Resurrection of Our Lord.* London: Macmillan, 1884.

Moberly, R. C. *Atonement and Personality.* London: John Murray, 1909.

Morris, Leon. *The Gospel According to John.* Grand Rapids: Eerdmans, 1971.

Murray, Andrew. *The True Vine.* Chicago: Moody Press (24th printing), 1982.

Nestle-Aland, *Novum Testamentum Graece.* 26th ed. Stuttgart: Deutsche Bibelstiftung, 1979. (Abbreviated as NA[26])

Newman, Barclay, and Eugene Nida. *A Translator's Handbook on the Gospel of John.* New York: United Bible Societies, 1980.

Pink, A. W. *Exposition of the Gospel of John.* 1945. Reprint, Grand Rapids: Zondervan, 1973.

Robertson, A. T. *Word Pictures in the Greek New Testament.* Nashville: Broadman Press, 1932.

Robinson, John A. T. *The Priority of John.* Oak Brook, Ill.: Meyer Stone Books, 1985.

Schnackenburg, Rudolph. *The Gospel According to St. John.* Translated by Kevin Smyth. New York: Crossroad, 1982.

Scholes, Robert, and Robert Kellogg. *The Nature of Narrative.* Oxford: Oxford University Press, 1966.

Staley, Jeffrey L. *The Print's First Kiss: A Rhetorical Investigation of the Implied Reader in the Fourth Gospel.* Atlanta: Scholars Press, 1988.

Vincent, Marvin R. *Word Studies in the New Testament.* 1887. Reprint, Grand Rapids: Eerdmans, 1946.

Westcott, B. F. *Gospel According to St. John.* 1881. Reprint, Grand Rapids: Zondervan, 1973.

Westcott, B. F., and Fenton Hort. *Introduction to the New Testament in the Original Greek* (with "Notes on Select Readings"). New York: Harper and Brothers, 1882.

Index of Scripture

Genesis

2:7   27, 90, 163
28:10–15   47
28:12   17
33:19   60
48:22   60

Exodus

3:1–18   83
3:6   86
12   43
12:14–20   107
12:46   17, 154
13:1–9   107
15:17   131
17:6   77
21   156
33:15   183
33:18   39
33:20   39
40:34   37

Leviticus

3:17   72
7:26–27   72
14:12–13   43
14:21   43
14:24   43
17:10–14   72
23:21   66
26:12   38

Numbers

6:12   43
7:10–11   98
9:12   154
21:6–9   56
21:8   56
27:16–17   94

Deuteronomy

2:14   66
11:26–29   60
11:26–29   61
12:5   61
17:7   67
18:15–18   42
18:15–18   46
18:15–18   68
18:15–18   70
18:18   48
19:15   67
27:1–8   60
27:1–8   61
28:6   94

Joshua

24:32   60

2 Samuel

7:12–14   48
7:12–16   80
13:23   105
15:23   148

1 Kings

8:63   98

2 Kings

1   42

2 Chronicles

6:6   61
7:12   61
13:19   105

Ezra

4:1–6   60
6:16   98

Job

23:10   180

Psalms

2   189n7
2:2   48
2:6   47, 48
2:7   47, 48, 53
16:9–10   53
22:18   17, 154
34:20   154
35   134
36:9   188n8
41   116
41:9   17, 116
69:4   134

203

Subject Index